NEW RELIGIOUS I
A GUIDE FOR THE

Continuum *Guides for the Perplexed*

Continuum's Guides for the Perplexed are clear, concise and accessible introductions to thinkers, writers and subjects that students and readers can find especially challenging. Concentrating specifically on what it is that makes the subject difficult to grasp, these books explain and explore key themes and ideas, guiding the reader towards a thorough understanding of demanding material.

***Guides for the Perplexed* available from Continuum:**

NEW RELIGIOUS MOVEMENTS: A GUIDE FOR THE PERPLEXED

PAUL OLIVER

continuum

Continuum International Publishing Group

The Tower Building	80 Maiden Lane
11 York Road	Suite 704
London	New York
SE1 7NX	NY 10038

www.continuumbooks.com

© Paul Oliver 2012

British Library Cataloguing-in-Publication Data
A catalogue record for this book is available from the British Library.

ISBN: HB: 978-1-4411-2553-8
PB: 978-1-4411-0197-6

Library of Congress Cataloging-in-Publication Data
A catalog record for this book is available from the Library of Congress.

Typeset by Newgen Imaging Systems Pvt Ltd, Chennai, India
Printed and bound in India

To Grace India

CONTENTS

PART I

PHILOSOPHICAL ISSUES AND NEW RELIGIOUS MOVEMENTS

CHAPTER 1

CONCEPTUAL ANALYSIS AND NEW RELIGIOUS MOVEMENTS

This chapter examines some philosophical and conceptual issues associated with new religious movements. It explores ways in which we might clarify concepts such as 'cult', 'sect', 'denomination' and 'new religious movement'. Some typologies of religious movements are analysed, along with issues involving the joining and leaving of new religious movements.

THE ORIGIN OF RELIGIOUS MOVEMENTS

If we consider for a moment the major religions of the world today, some appear to have gradually evolved, while others were founded by a specific individual. Hinduism and Shinto would appear to be examples of the former category. It is very difficult to establish even an approximate date for their origin, and even more difficult to associate their establishment with a specific, named human being. On the other hand Christianity and Sikhism are examples of religions which we can date fairly precisely, and for which we are familiar with the identity of their founder.

In the case of religions with a specific founder, sociologists would be very interested in explanations for the survival of such religions. After all, they could very easily have declined once their founder died. Sociologists would probably point to a combination of factors, political, social and perhaps economic, which combined to create a fertile ground for the religion to grow and flourish. It is possible perhaps, that a religion requires a critical mass of adherents in order to sustain its existence, and to expand. Indeed it seems perhaps a little surprising that there are in the world so few major religions.

Although there is little extant evidence to support this, it seems reasonable to suppose that throughout history, many religions must have been started by different people, but for a variety of reasons did not manage to become established. They would have faded away after different periods of time. Some might have been offshoots of existing faiths, while others might have represented an innovative system of spiritual thought. It is, of course, very interesting to hypothesize about the factors which might have caused their decline. Certainly, there are plenty of historical examples of one religion or denomination not being able to tolerate another and embarking upon a period of persecution. The dominant faith would typically destroy any religious records of the minority faith, which at least partially explains the relatively little evidence of minority religions throughout history.

Prior to the rise of Christianity in Europe there would have existed a range of belief systems which have been loosely designated as pagan or shamanistic. We do have some evidence of these, for example, in the writings of Roman historians, but the general antipathy towards them within the growing Christian society led to their marginalization and decline. It is also interesting to note the terminology applied by the dominant religion in this case to that of the other minority faiths. They were described using the epithet 'pagan', signifying the religion or religions of rather unsophisticated people who lived in the remoter countryside. It is a clearly pejorative term from the beginning and has largely remained so.

The development of new religions is not, therefore, a new phenomenon, but has probably existed since before historical records. However, there has been an apparent expansion in the number of new religions during the latter half of the twentieth century and into the present century. The development of mass media for communications, and certainly the advent of the internet, has provided a mechanism for the expansion of new religions. Using these new media, religions can disseminate their spiritual teachings throughout the world; they can recruit new members on a global scale and can more easily attract financial support for the organization. It is, however, difficult to estimate the number of new religions which exist in the world at the moment (Lewis, 2004). One of the major difficulties lies in problems of definition. A 'new' religion may in fact be rather similar to an existing mainstream faith and not represent a belief system which is in any way radically different. On the other hand, a new movement may be very clearly an alternative spirituality and be part of what one might term the religion counter-culture. In addition, as Lewis indicates, members of traditional religions may share at least some of the interests of members of new religious movements.

Moreover, computer-based communication has enabled people to be familiar with a wide range of spiritual beliefs. Indeed as Chryssides (1996, p. 2) points out, 'they can at least savour something of the spiritual practices, without even having to seek out the organization.' In the early part of the twentieth century most people were only familiar with the religion of their immediate community. It was the natural thing for children to be educated within that religion and then to practise that faith for life. However, in the contemporary world, through the medium of our computers, we can become familiar with a wide range of spiritual beliefs and practices. People can be much less reliant upon the faith into which they were born, and can select a different religious philosophy, whether one of the main religions of the world or a new minority religion. The way in which we make sense of this enormous variety of potential religious experience is, however, far from clear; and one of the key issues is the kind of language we will use to describe new religions.

THE CONCEPT OF A NEW RELIGION

The concepts that we use in religious discourse, like those in other areas of human life, reflect the way in which we think about the world. In formulating our concepts concerning new religions we may, for example, concentrate on the mechanism whereby a religion separates from a larger belief system, and begins to exist autonomously. On the other hand, in the case of a completely novel religion, we may concentrate upon the social process of its formation. Alternatively, we may focus upon the age of a new movement, concluding that after the lapse of a certain period of time a 'new' religion need no longer be considered 'new'. The most popular term that is employed in academic circles (and indeed in the title of this book) is 'new religious movements', but there is little general consensus about which new movements should be included within this category. In other words, we have a concept or term, but without any precise defining criteria. The terms 'sect' and 'cult' are nowadays used relatively infrequently in the study of religion, although they may still occur in other disciplines. The concept 'sect' is generally employed for a religious movement which has broken away from the originating faith but retains a relatively orthodox set of practices. On the other hand, the term 'cult' is usually employed for a completely new religious movement which is largely unrelated to anything that has previously existed. The term could be applied, for example, to the Heaven's Gate organization, which believed that members would pass to a more desirable location in the universe by means of a spaceship that would collect them from Earth. In furtherance of these aims, the group committed mass suicide in 1997.

It is interesting that the terms cult and sect were in the past widely used in academic discourse, but also became accepted and understood by the general public. By and large, there was a shared understanding of the characteristics of such organizations. However, primarily due to adverse publicity in the media concerning the treatment of some cult members, the terms cult and sect acquired a pejorative connotation. This applied perhaps more to the term cult. Academics were eager to avoid the use of concepts that might appear biased, and hence adopted the term 'new religious movements', which was regarded as much more value-free. However, as noted above, the new term proved somewhat difficult to define conceptually, and it became far from clear which religious movements could be included within its terms of reference. In addition, the term was not readily adopted outside the academic world, and the general public either failed to understand it or used it sparingly. It is worth examining these terms in rather more detail in order to evaluate them for academic and everyday use.

THE NATURE OF A CULT

The term cult has tended to be used for an organization on the margins of mainstream religious belief. Whether we consider its doctrines or belief system, its ritual and practice, or features of its social organization, a cult is usually marked by significant differences from the principal established faiths. It is normally unusual for such a differentiated organization to arise through an evolutionary process, and hence cults are often associated with a founding figure who has been able to influence potential members through some features of their personality. David Koresh, the leader of the Branch Davidian movement at the time of the Waco siege in 1993, apparently possessed an extremely detailed knowledge of the Bible, and was able to use his ability to draw upon Biblical quotations to influence members. The leaders or founders of cults have also been noted for their charisma. While in essence a value-neutral quality, charisma has certainly acquired a negative connotation in the case of cult leaders. It has been associated with the capacity to sway potential recruits into joining an organization, and once members, to make considerable financial contributions. Charismatic leaders have also been associated with indoctrinating cult members into extreme beliefs, and persuading them to adopt patterns of behaviour which might commonly be regarded as socially abnormal. One should not assume, however, that all leaders of cults or new religious organizations act in this dominating or controlling way. Thus in relation to the Neopagan religion Wicca, Wagar (2009, p. 7) points out that 'its rituals and practices and its theology are evolving from a community of believers' experiences rather than a prophet's individual inspiration.'

It has been asserted, for example, that one strategy employed by cult leaders has been to isolate new members from their families and former friends. This has the result that new cult members make new friends within the organization and are restricted in terms of social contacts with other cult members. One consequence of this is that in terms of evaluating new religious ideas, their only terms of reference are the other members of the cult. It is not possible for new members to compare the ideas of the organization with comparable ideas in other organizations. In other words, the cult is a closed society and can be very disorienting for members. In everyday life we rely very much on being exposed to a range of ideas and opinions in order to maintain a sense of perspective, and without this variety of thought, we are likely to be more easily persuaded to believe things we would not normally accept as valid. To use an oft-quoted word in relation to cults, we are likely to be 'brainwashed' (Richardson and Introvigne, 2001).

The public disquiet about cults tends often to centre upon the alleged lack of autonomy for its members. This erosion of the self-determination of members can lead to exploitation of various kinds. This might be financial exploitation, sexual exploitation or a more generalized tendency to use people for the benefit of the group and perhaps significantly for the benefit of the group leaders. The encouragement of such a lack of autonomy is unethical because the capacity to reflect upon issues and then to take rational decisions for oneself is arguably a significant feature of what it means to be human. This lack of autonomy is frequently accompanied by a requirement to conform closely to the doctrines, ideology and social customs of the group. That which is perceived as acceptably conforming to the norms of the group is very often determined by the leader. In extreme cases such conformity can be extremely damaging to members, either psychologically or physically. Perhaps the archetypal example of such conformity is the case of the Peoples Temple, whose members were either forced, or at least persuaded to commit mass suicide by the policies and autocratic approach of the leader, the Reverend Jim Jones.

The notion of a profound commitment to a cult on the part of members is often cited as a characteristic of such organizations. The nature of such commitment has been studied by Cosgel (2001). There may be many reasons for a deep sense of commitment within religious movements, and some organizations may set out to deliberately induce such feelings in order to secure group cohesion. Some movements may seek to create a sense of isolation in a member, in order that the only relationships formed are those within the group. In this way, the member may be extremely reluctant to consider leaving the movement for fear of losing all existing friends and contacts.

It is worth noting, however, that even though some so-called cults do exhibit some of these patterns of organizational control, it is not necessarily typical of all of them. There is enormous variation in the structure, doctrine and practice of new religious movements, and generalization is difficult. Although some may adopt practices which render them very different from orthodox religious traditions, the use of a word such as 'deviant' to describe them is, to some degree, problematic. There are so many variants, even in orthodox religions, that it is difficult to determine normative criteria by which to judge a movement, which is sufficiently different, to be termed deviant.

Some cults are associated with heretical beliefs. For the term heresy to be applied to a cult, however, the latter would have to subscribe to an amended version of a mainstream theology. For example, if a group did not subscribe to a basic tenet of the Christian faith, then they might be accused of heresy by the Christian Church and labelled a cult. Those who criticize cults most strongly, however, are generally less concerned with theological issues, than with the extent to which an organization is controlling of its members and employs various forms of indoctrination.

The organizations which are critical of cults are generally described as anti-cult movements, although the term embraces a wide range of different organizations. Moreover, it is possible to distinguish the 'anti-cult movement' from the 'counter-cult movement' (Cowan, 2002). In the early years of the twentieth century, there was a tendency for mainstream Christian Churches to challenge some of the newer Christian groups such as Jehovah's Witnesses on the grounds of theological belief. The latter were generally considered to be heretical by the established Christian Churches, and strenuous attempts were made by the counter-cult movement to challenge their belief system, and to draw the attention of the general public to what were perceived as their doctrinal errors.

The anti-cult movement, however, was a predominantly secular organization, whereas the counter-cult movement had a Christian focus. The anti-cult movement developed in the 1960s and 1970s as a response to the increasing number of particularly young people who joined one or the other of the new religious movements which were proliferating at the time. Members of the anti-cult movement were often originally parents, relatives or friends of young people who had joined what were seen as 'cults'. Gradually these organizations of parents and friends developed into major organizations with considerable influence. They were concerned about a number of issues involving cults including the allegedly unethical ways in which young people were recruited, isolated from friends and relatives, persuaded to make financial contributions and/or to work extremely hard for the religious movement. In general, the anti-cult movement was concerned about the degree of control exerted on young people, and in particular the allegation that young people were often brainwashed by the organization. The movement was secular because it was really concerned with groups of any religious background, if they demonstrated some of the above tendencies which appeared to typify cults. The anti-cult movement also focused upon the procedure whereby a member could leave a new religious movement. In the past, there had been accusations that in some cults members were in effect prevented from leaving, and the anti-cult movement tried to develop strategies to help members who wished to leave the cult. Anti-cult movements tried to collect data of various types concerning the nature of life inside cults, to varying degrees of success. One of their principal strategies was to interview apostates who had become disenchanted with the cult, and who in some cases were willing to outline what they saw as undesirable practices within the cult.

It is interesting that on the one hand some academics feel that the term 'cult' is inappropriate to use, because it has acquired negative connotations, while on the other hand others consider that these pejorative connotations are a social construction, and are not an intrinsic element of the concept. York (1996, p. 10) argues for the retention of the term, and suggests that 'like the sect, the cult is merely an indicator of deviant, non-traditional or non-mainstream behaviour.' One of the distinct advantages of the term cult is that it is generally well-understood in the world at large, and most non-academics appreciate the nuances of the concept in terms of charismatic leadership or potential exploitation, for example. Indeed, it is these very pejorative associations of the concept which make it useful in academic analysis. It is of course true that the concept is not neutral and objective, but it is the very subjectivity, and value-laden nature of the term, which makes it useful in discussing new religious organizations. There is an alternative school of thought that places an emphasis upon the need to employ objective terms, and hence prefers such concepts as 'alternative spiritualities' or 'new religious movements'. However, their very neutrality does, according to some, make them less useful for academic discussion. There is also the argument that no concept is free from value judgements, and hence can be called truly objective.

A major point of debate concerning cults has been the nature of the recruitment or conversion process on the one hand, and on the other hand, the freedom members have to leave an organization if they become unhappy with their lives there. It has been argued that people join cults for a multiplicity of reasons, including straightforward friendship and companionship, quite apart from any feelings of commitment to a particular ideology. Many new members are young people, and this can perhaps be explained by their not having yet established a stable pattern of life, and their attraction to an organization which is friendly and welcoming. Stark and Bainbridge (1996) have produced one of the most influential analyses of the process of becoming affiliated to a cult, while Bader and Demaris (1996) have subjected their analysis to critical scrutiny. The autonomy with which members can leave a cult remains a significant test of the ethics of an organization. The exertion of any pressure to remain a member would constitute a significant criticism of the organization of a new religious movement.

The attitudes of individual governments to cults remain varied. Governments are influenced by a number of factors when considering their approach to cults and when considering the possibility of legislation in this area. On the one hand, governments are concerned to maintain the principle of freedom of religious expression, and given the prevalence of equal opportunities legislation, generally would not wish to be viewed as limiting the freedoms of its citizens. On the other hand, governments had to take into account claims of exploitation by individual members of cults, but more significantly, the well-publicized, tragic endings of some cults through mass suicide and/or murder. The deaths of members of the Order of the Solar Temple, between 1994 and 1997, are a well-known example. Not only that, but certain new religious movements have become very wealthy and influential organizations with considerable power in terms of lobbying for their own interests. Some movements clearly cannot be viewed as merely temporary, minority collections of individuals representing unusual or eccentric opinion. They are substantial organizations which have demanded to be treated seriously by government. Nevertheless, it is perhaps to be expected that different governments, perhaps influenced by events on their own soil, have reacted differently to the phenomenon of new religious movements.

The Commission on New Religious Movements (1998) established by the Swedish government published a report which while noting some caution was broadly positive about the phenomenon of new religious movements. The report noted that in the commission's view there was evidence that many members of such movements enjoyed and learned from their membership of the organization, and that generally, when they decided to leave, this was not a traumatic experience. The United States also has a reputation for being broadly supportive of new religious movements, and indeed has a great diversity of such movements. The overall official attitude in Germany and France has been rather more sceptical about new religious movements. The attitude in France may have been at least partly conditioned by the deaths within the Order of the Solar Temple, whose leader Jo Di Mambro was French. The French government established a Commission on Cults in 1995, which was followed in 2005 by a Prime Ministerial statement advocating the need to monitor cults. In 2006 a further Commission of Enquiry was established to concentrate in particular on the effects of cults on children. In general, one can argue that there has been something of a contrast between the approach of the United States and that of Europe to the question of cults.

SECTS AND DENOMINATIONS

The term 'sect', usually considered to be derived from the Latin meaning 'to follow', is a religious group which has typically broken away from the associated main religion or denomination. The original cause of the separation may have been a theological or doctrinal difference. Often however, a sect still adheres to most of the key belief systems of the originating faith. On occasion, the sect founders may have felt that the original religion was not adhering sufficiently closely to the main principles of the faith, and hence the development of a schism. In this case the new religious movement is perhaps trying to sustain the fundamentals of the religion. Nevertheless a typical sect will differ significantly from the original religion in order to differentiate it in terms of either practice or belief. A sect may either evolve slowly or may be founded by an influential individual. It may retain its own identity or may evolve slowly into a new denomination or church. A denomination is a larger group than a sect, and one which may have evolved over an extended period of time. There may be only minor differences with the parent religion, but these may be sufficient to maintain the distinctiveness of the denomination. The Protestant churches within Christianity, for example, may be considered as denominations. Some people may consider a sect as being a variant of a cult, although generally the two are distinguishable. Both will, for example, incorporate new and different ideas within their belief system, but the sect will generally retain some commonalities with an originating religion. Wilson (1993) has analysed a number of religious movements discussing the extent to which they may be considered as sects. In relation to the Seventh-day Adventist Church, for example, he points out that there are some indications, such as its organizational structure, which might support the argument of its becoming a denomination. On the other hand, argues Wilson, there would appear to remain some significant differences, notably in terms of the way members conduct their lives, that suggests it is more accurate to think of it as a sect. These distinctions are, however, very difficult to make, and it remains a difficult conceptual question to distinguish cults, sects and denominations.

A case in point would be the Theosophical Society, an organization with a considerable history and associated with celebrated names in the study of spirituality. Trevithick (2008, p. 1) refers to it as a cult, and also raises some questions about the manner in which young people were recruited to the movement. Nevertheless, the question of terminology remains ambivalent. One of the events that can initiate divisions in a movement is the death of a leader, leading ultimately to the development of new movements. Healy (2010) discusses such events in the case of Swami Muktananda and his Siddha Yoga movement. Healy uses the term 'schism' to refer to such divisions.

NEW RELIGIOUS MOVEMENTS

One of the issues emerging from the previous discussion is that it is both difficult to define terms such as cult and sect very precisely, and therefore problematic when trying to draw conceptual boundaries around the types of organizations which are being considered. In addition, the nuances attached to these terms when they are in popular use makes it somewhat difficult to employ them in academic debate. Attempts have been made to identify other terms which on the one hand are more objective, and on the other, occupy a more precise conceptual territory. 'Alternative spirituality' is one such term. The use of 'spirituality' helps to embrace the very wide nature of the belief systems discussed, while the adjective 'alternative' suggests movements which provide a contrast to established, organized religions. However, 'new religious movements' has become the preferred term in academic circles.

This term has the advantage for academics that it appears to have retained an independence of any value judgements or connotations, which is advantageous in much writing on religious studies. While the term has succeeded in becoming well-disseminated throughout the world of scholarship, it does not appear to have attracted the same usage in everyday speech and language. This can be a difficulty in terms of making academic discussion on the subject more widely available and understood. There is also some ambiguity concerning the constituent words of the term. The word 'new' could be construed as referring to movements which are new simply in relation to long established organized religions, without assuming any implication of the actual date of development. On the other hand, the word may be rather more commonly taken to indicate a movement which has developed in more recent history or even in contemporary times. This can then involve debate over a historical demarcation line, before which movements might not generally be included. Contemporary writing seems to indicate a variety of practice in this regard. For the purposes of the present work, those movements discussed in some detail in the main body of the book have evolved largely since the Second World War. In other parts of the book, where just a passing reference is made to movements for purposes of illustration a more general interpretation of 'newness' is employed, along with practical considerations of whether a movement is generally discussed within the literature on new religious movements.

The reason for taking the Second World War as a historical dividing line is that there were enormous social changes after this event including in the nature of religious belief and practice. The movement of people and communities both during and after the war led to a rapidly growing awareness of different religions and cultures. This facilitated not only the possibility of interest in religions other than that in which one had been reared, but also the possibility of conversion. Additionally, this atmosphere of the mixing of religions provided a fertile ground for the development of new religions, either by a process of fragmentation from existing faiths or by the creation of a completely new movement. The Second World War thus provides a practical and useful dividing line, between a period of relative stability in terms of religious development and the subsequent period of innovation and change.

The word 'religion' in new religious movements, while not creating enormous conceptual problems, may also raise some questions of which movements to include and which to exclude from discussion. The relatively recent development of movements associated with humanistic psychology or with phenomenology or existentialism may raise questions about whether such views of personal development are better considered as a religion. The New Age movement is perhaps another case in point, where a range of mystical, spiritual practices are combined with environmental sensitivities and communal living and travelling. In addition, a range of lifestyle and personal development practices combine to create a movement which while undoubtedly possessing a religious dimension is also to some extent secularized. Practices in terms of a definition vary in the literature, and there is no real a priori reason why we should aspire to a precise dividing line. While it may be appealing to have precise criteria by which to judge whether an organization be included within the conceptual territory of new religious movements, academic enquiry is rarely as neat as this. It is often more usual to find a certain vagueness in the dividing lines between concepts, rather than an absolute precision. Indeed, even when considering the main religions of the world, some would argue that there are no precise divisions. Geaves (1996) pointed out in a study of religion in the Punjab that the assumed clear distinctions between Hinduism and Sikhism were not necessarily reflected in the religious life of the Punjab villages. In reality, members of the two religious communities would sometimes attend the same temple. There existed, in effect, considerable overlap in some areas of religious belief and practice.

STUDY QUESTION

Another dimension to the term new religious movement involves the situation where a major faith, which is normally associated with certain countries and cultures, becomes established within a different culture. The rapid expansion of interest in Buddhism in the West is an example of this. In some cases, the new organization may be treated as a new religious movement, even though it is clearly still associated with the originating faith. The Triratna Buddhist Community is arguably an example of such a situation. On the other hand there are some Theravada groups which have attempted to recreate a Buddhist context from a different culture as closely as possible. Amaravati Buddhist Centre, part of the English Sangha Trust, which is based upon Buddhist practice in Thailand, is an example, although in general this would probably not be termed a new religious movement.

When a religion from one culture is deliberately initiated and developed in a different culture, what criteria could be used to decide whether it should be treated as a new religious movement?

Other new religious movements are derived from very ancient traditions, which did not survive in their original form. Paganism, for example, is a rather eclectic term for probably a very wide range of belief systems which flourished in pre-Roman Europe and elsewhere. These nature-based religions fell victim to a variety of oppressive practices and persecution, until they ceased to exist in any meaningful sense. They have, however, been resurrected in modern times as neopaganism, and very often discussed within the terms of a new religious movement. In this case, the term 'new' simply suggests that an ancient tradition has been brought to life again, using any available sources to establish a contemporary version as close to the original as possible.

CATEGORIZING NEW RELIGIOUS MOVEMENTS

It is perhaps little surprising that with a concept as difficult to define as new religious movements, it can prove equally problematic to place the many existing movements into meaningful categories. Various scholars have tried to identify appropriate categories, and have generally opted for fairly broad themes within which to place different movements.

Wallis (1984), for example, categorized some movements as 'world-rejecting' and others as 'world-affirming'. Those movements that reject the world are broadly considered to hold the view that the world is materialistic and secular, and generally antagonistic to the spiritual life. It is thought to be difficult to maintain a religious life and still be in contact with the material world. Hence there is a tendency for such movements to withdraw from the world as much as possible, and to lead an independent spiritual life. On the other hand, those movements which affirm the world are perceived as being able to combine the spiritual life with an existence within contemporary society. Members of such groups, while perhaps not accepting all of the values of secular society, are generally able to continue with their spiritual lives within such a context. There is also seen as being an intermediate category of those movements which adapt to the world, while at the same time neither rejecting nor affirming it.

Typologies such as this may also be used to monitor the nature of change in new religious movements. As Björkqvist (1990) argues, change is very much inherent in religious movements, and particularly in terms of the relationship between the movement and the society within which it has developed. Björkqvist uses the typology of Wallis, among others, to analyse the nature of change within several Hindu-oriented groups.

In a different mode of categorization, Hargrove (1978) proposed a typology based on the concept of 'integrative' and 'transformative' religions. She conceived the former as possessing many of the features of a sect, in that they very often developed from established faiths, and tended to have a sound organization and relatively orthodox ethical values. On the other hand, new religious movements, which were categorized as transformative, tended to be much more concerned with the subjective spiritual development of individual members, and the way in which they decided to change their lifestyle and world view. With any sort of typology it is rarely easy to place individual cases within a category with any degree of certainty. With regard to new religious movements, the latter are so complex that this is even more difficult. However, the advantage of employing a typology is that it does encourage us to reflect upon the key features and characteristics of a movement, in order to compare it rationally with others.

JOINING AND LEAVING NEW RELIGIOUS MOVEMENTS

The most sensitive aspects of the new religious movements include on the one hand the strategies which they employ in order to gain converts, and on the other, the ease with which members may leave the organization if that is their wish. Those who are antagonistic to new movements have generally argued that coercive or duplicitous methods were employed to attract potential converts, and that once established as members or converts, they found it very difficult to leave the movement, if they so desired. During the 1960s and early 1970s, probably a period of rapid expansion in the number of new religious movements, it appeared that the majority of converts were young people in their teens or twenties. The argument followed from this that they were more suggestible and capable of being persuaded to join a new organization. Moreover, this was an age during which young people were still developing an individual world view, and hence were perhaps likely to be interested in an organization which presented a novel way of looking at the world. Equally, they might be more easily persuaded that to leave the organization would be a mistake. However, more recent research (Lewis, 2006) suggests that in contemporary society, those who join new religious movements are more likely to be in their thirties than twenties, and hence arguably more resistant to persuasion to join organizations.

In relation to the concept of 'conversion' some people have argued that in some ways it is an inappropriate term, since the process of deciding to participate in a religious movement may be very complex. Some of the members of the Sai Baba movement interviewed by Exon (1995) spoke more of a coming-together of the potential convert and the organization, rather than a conversion process involving active intervention by existing members. This suggests a much less persuasive process than is normally imagined, with potential members exercising their own autonomy.

In a similar vein, Harrington (2000) studied the conversion process among Wiccans, and found a general sense of rejection of the term 'conversion'. Wiccans tended to argue that the process of 'conversion' was much more one of acceptance that the Wiccan belief system and spirituality was already a part of them. The process of 'conversion' was a recognition of this state, and a full acceptance that the person would feel much more at home among other Wiccans. This idea thus tends to argue against the notion that new religious movements, and particularly those referred to as cults, are principally concerned with persuading people to join their organization by one means or another.

It is, therefore, clear that for many people the experience of being a part of a new religious movement is a positive one, and that such new movements are part of a contemporary world which encourages the acceptance of diversity in terms of religious belief and practice. Dawson (1998, p. 139) pointed out that 'the new religious consciousness is remarkably more syncretistic, accepting of relativism, and tolerant of other religious perspectives . . .', and new religious movements have added much to this liberal viewpoint.

FURTHER READING

Bainbridge, W. S. (1997) *The Sociology of Religious Movements*, London: Routledge.

Dawson, L. L. (ed.) (2004) *Cults and New Religious Movements: A Reader*, Oxford: Blackwell.

Hunt, S. (2003) *Alternative Religions: A Sociological Introduction*, Aldershot: Ashgate.

Lynch, G. (2007) *New Spirituality: An Introduction to Belief beyond Religion*, London: I.B. Tauris.

Saliba, J. A. (1995) *Perspectives on New Religious Movements*, London: Geoffrey Chapman.

CHAPTER 2

APPLICATION OF CONCEPTS TO
NEW RELIGIOUS MOVEMENTS

The aim of this chapter is to relate a wide range of new religious movements to the concepts analysed in the previous chapter. In this way it is hoped to illustrate the scope of new movements, that is, those derived from traditional faiths as well as the ones which have arisen independently.

THE ATTRACTION OF NEW RELIGIOUS MOVEMENTS

Most, but not all, major religions possess a distinct aspect of their theology, which concerns a major, hypothetical event that is assumed to take place in the future. One of the most famous such predictions is the 'second coming' of Jesus within the Christian faith. Other religions, including Hinduism, which conceive of the universe and of time as operating in cycles of extremely long duration, think of the replacement of one period by another. Each period of time is conceived as being characterized by certain features, whether for the better or worse. The transition from one period to another is seen as an extremely important event in the future. The study of such important future events in religion is termed eschatology.

A number of new religious movements, and perhaps in particular those which may be characterized as cults, have eschatological predictions within their world view. These can be very influential in persuading new members to join a cult, and indeed may be used by cult leaders to stress the importance and significance of their particular movement. After all, if a religious leader can argue that a particular movement gives special insights into a major spiritual event in the future, then the movement could be seen as of considerable importance.

An example of eschatological belief is millennialism or the belief that humanity is destined to experience a thousand years of peace and spiritual tranquillity. This is often thought of within Christianity as the coming of the millennium, a 1,000-year period during which the spirit and teachings of Jesus Christ will prevail in the world. Such millennial teachings have been adopted in a variety of secular contexts, including within political teachings, where social change is seen as bringing about a new world order. The 'millennium' is often seen in religious contexts as a period of spiritual peace after which evil and negative forces will be destroyed, bringing a final and permanent state of Godliness to the world. Christians might refer to this as the coming of the Kingdom of God.

A different eschatological belief is the notion of an apocalypse or dramatic event in the future, which will cause the end of the world or of civilization. Such apocalyptic notions are found in some new religious movements, often accompanied by the teaching that the new movement can provide a strategy to escape from the consequences of the apocalypse. For those considering joining a new religious movement, such an idea can prove very seductive, for it can make them feel that they, and only they, have access to a special form of salvation. Bendle (2005, p. 2) in analysing the nature of apocalyptic ideas in popular culture has also argued that puritan groups in coming to America found '... it was the New Jerusalem – the city on the hill that was a beacon to all people who pursued the righteousness of God'.

An example of a millennial belief which has had considerable effect upon a number of new religious movements is that of the existence of unidentified flying objects (UFOs). The general characteristics of UFO belief systems is that there exist either in other parts of our solar system, or further away in other galaxies, advanced civilizations which have made contact with Earth. These contacts continue to take place, and the assumption is that the intervention of such civilizations will generally have a benign effect on us, and will indeed help to create a utopian world in which hunger, warfare and disease are a thing of the past. These civilizations will be able to achieve this, so it is believed, because of their much more sophisticated technology, culture and social systems. Of course, there is no *a priori* rationale for the assumption that the intervention of intergalactic powers would necessarily be benign. It is equally plausible that advanced space civilizations may wish to colonize the Earth. If a new religious movement were to base its belief system on such an assumption, then it would be better described as apocalyptic, rather than millennial.

A new religion which can probably best be described as millennial in nature is the Aetherius Society. This organization was founded in 1955 by George King who claimed that he had received a communication from a power on the planet Venus, who used the name 'Aetherius'. King had a strong interest in the mystical, and particularly in yoga. King, who died in 1997, was regarded with great reverence by the members of the society, and this sense of respect has continued after his death. The society is well-organized, and has achieved recognition as a legitimate body in a number of countries (Saliba, 1999, p. 4). The Aetherius Society regards George King as a spiritual Master, and believes that eventually a successor to him will arrive on Earth from outer space. This arrival will indicate the start of a new era or millennium of peace and spiritual advancement. There is no specific understanding of when this arrival will take place, but in the meantime one of the purposes of the Society is to prepare for this by leading a good and spiritual life.

Many of the beliefs of the Society appear to have a great deal in common with other mainstream religions. The principal aim of the Society is to stress the importance of acting in order to benefit the rest of humanity. One of the main ways in which this is achieved is that members try to radiate spiritual energy, particularly focusing it towards areas where it is perceived to be necessary. There is a general belief in the unity of all religions, to the extent that they are all considered to possess an element of truth, and are striving towards the same goal. There is, however, a range of beliefs concerning the existence and nature of extraterrestrial intelligence. The great religious teachers of the main world faiths are assumed to have come from outer space, and the existence of UFOs is unequivocally accepted as true. Although many people will find it difficult to accept seriously the doctrines concerning visits from outer space, nevertheless the religious tolerance and humanity demonstrated by the Society will no doubt be seen by many as an attractive feature.

Raëlism is another example of a UFO movement. To be rather more precise, Raëlism asserts that all of human life on Earth is the creation of a society from outer space, whose creatures are similar in broad structure to human beings. Indeed, the underlying reason for this is that they decided to create human beings specifically in their own form. The members of this civilization are considered by Raëlians to be extremely advanced technologically, with a profound understanding of biological engineering. This knowledge of biomedical processes enabled them to construct the human race. The Raëlians termed this space society, the Elohim.

The movement was started in 1974 by a Frenchman named Claude Vorilhon, who later assumed the name Raël. He claimed that members of the Elohim had made contact with him, and explained that they had been familiar with the planet Earth for a long time. Indeed they had maintained contact since before the establishment of the main religions of the world. The Elohim had specifically sent the main teachers and prophets of the main religions, so that they could pass on some of the teachings of the Elohim, which were relevant to a particular period in human history. Having done this, Raëlians argue that the Elohim did not interact any further with the Earth, in order to give human beings the time and space to develop as a culture. We have now passed into the Age of Revelation, a period of time in which human beings can now become informed about the role of the Elohim. To the extent that Raëlians believe that humans have now reached an age of enlightenment, it seems reasonable to think of Raëlism as a millennial organization.

Raëlism is not particularly inclusive in terms of other faiths, and indeed new members must declare that they reject other religions. There is a hierarchical structure of seven different levels within the religion, with the possibility of advance from one level to another. In terms of ethics, the movement can probably be described as relativistic, with members encouraged to act in a way which seems appropriate at the time. The latest venture of the organization is to encourage the Elohim to visit the Earth in substantial numbers. In order to achieve this, the organization wishes to establish an 'Embassy' which would act as a focus for the arriving Elohim. The movement has gone so far as to invite interested countries to propose themselves as a site for the Raël Embassy.

Both the Aetherius Society and Raëlism can best be described as millennial, in the sense that they look forward to a beneficial period in world history, when human beings will lead a peaceful, benign existence. However, some UFO groups are apocalyptic in the sense that they predict a cataclysmic event at some stage in the future, and that usually members of the organization in questions will survive, or have a far better experience that non-members. Therein lies at least the partial attraction of such groups.

God's Salvation Church, or Chen Tao, is an example of such a group. The leader of the movement, Hon-Ming Chen predicted in the 1990s that the world would be caught up in a cataclysmic nuclear war, which he referred to as 'the Great Tribulation'. He predicted that this would occur in 1999 and that God would return in a flying saucer to rescue members of Chen Tao (Prather, 1999, p. 15). We can therefore think of Chen Tao as an apocalyptic religion, linked to UFO beliefs.

Chen Tao was established initially in Taiwan, but Hon-Ming Chen felt that a more propitious location for the movement would be the United States. The members of the movement eventually settled in the town of Garland, in Texas, in 1997. The group achieved some considerable fame and notoriety by the claim of their leader that God would come down to earth on 31 March 1998 and appear across the United States on Channel 18 television. When this did not happen, Hon-Ming Chen made some public announcements, but did not apparently try to re-interpret the failed prophecy with some new cosmological explanation. In 1999 the remaining members of the movement left Texas for New York State. Although there were fears, particularly among the police and inhabitants of Garland, that the group might be dangerous, or even participate in collective suicide, the overall behaviour of the group members appears to have been eccentric, rather than a danger to themselves or others. It would not seem unreasonable if people were to apply the term cult to this movement, although one does not gain the impression that the leader was unduly manipulative, or that members were restricted in their actions, as is suggested with some groups.

The prediction of a highly desirable spiritual event has a long history within new religious movements. One of the most persuasive of these predictions, particularly among Christians, has been the idea that Jesus Christ would return to earth and create a divine 'kingdom'. This philosophy of the 'Second Coming' was the central doctrine of the Millerites, an American-based movement established in the early nineteenth century.

The founder of this movement was William Miller who lived in New York State, and was an ardent student of the Bible. He was not a trained theologian, but after extensive study and analysis of biblical texts, he decided that it was in principle possible to predict the approximate date of the Second Coming of Jesus. He determined that this would be approximately in 1843. Miller was fairly tentative in explaining his ideas to others, and initially there was not a great deal of interest. Gradually, however, particularly after an expanding campaign of publications on the subject, Miller's prediction began to attract enormous attention. His ideas were no longer causing interest around the New England area, but spread across the United States, and were carried overseas, largely by the force of the Millerite publications. Members of the movement continued to analyse biblical texts in order to try to refine the date of Christ's advent, and this was provisionally decided to be between March 1843 and March 1844. Eventually the date was revised by some members of the movement to be 22 October 1844.

There was clearly a high degree of anticipation for this date, but when Jesus did not appear, it was very difficult for members of the movement to know how to react. The date became known as the Great Disappointment. The Millerite movement could clearly not continue in its previous form, and several different groupings evolved, one of which would eventually develop into the Seventh-day Adventist Church. Many people, however, left the movement, unable to reconcile themselves with the failed prophecy.

Some might regard Millerism as a Christian sect, in that it developed from biblical studies, and that it was millennial in approach, in so far as it predicted a new period in world spiritual history. William Miller himself does not appear to belong to the stereotype of the sect leader, as somewhat manipulative or wishing to exert his own authority over others. Indeed it was a feature of his approach that he encouraged members of the movement to analyse the Bible for themselves, and to form their own judgements about the prophecy. The role and influence of leaders within such religious movements does, however, remain a source of interest and contention.

THE ORIGIN OF NEW RELIGIOUS MOVEMENTS

New religious movements start in a variety of ways. There may be a theological disagreement within an established faith which leads to a division, and the beginnings of a new movement. An individual may feel inspired to start a new religion, or one or more individuals may receive a form of spiritual revelation which motivates them to start a new movement. Cao Dai, a movement which started in Vietnam, is an example of the latter case.

Members of the movement tend to employ the term Cao Dai as a synonym for God, and it was through a divine revelation to Ngô Văn Chiêu and several others that the movement was started. The symbol of the religion, a single eye, was also revealed by God at approximately the same time. As a result of these revelations, the religion of Cao Dai was founded in 1926. In fact, Caodaists hold the view that God created the religion, through the medium of His revelation, rather than being a human-created faith.

Caodaism is a characteristically syncretistic movement. It believes very firmly in the equality of all religions. Although it accepts that religions are superficially different in terms of beliefs and customs, at the same time it asserts that all faiths are equivalent at a deeper level. Caodaists believe that God is the same in all faiths, even though different faiths may refer to God by different names and in different ways. This kind of philosophical approach tends to generate a sense of tolerance towards other belief systems, and also enables Cao Dai to draw upon teachings from different faiths, uniting them into a separate belief system. For example, Caodaism draws upon Hindu philosophy in order to incorporate doctrines of karma and moksha. The religion asserts that moral actions in this life will enable a person to enhance one's karma, which will bring rewards in future lives. The ultimate purpose of Cao Dai is that through a series of ethical lives, the individual person will be able to escape from the cycle of rebirth and to gain union with God. Caodaists practise meditation extensively as a technique designed to help unite the individual soul with the universal soul, or God. Broadly speaking Cao Dai draws upon a number of religions, including Taoism, Confucianism, Hinduism, Buddhism and Christianity, in order to create a synthesis of spiritual ideas. The earthly founders of Cao Dai based their authority upon the revelations which they received from God. In the case of some new religious movements, however, the founders of movements claim themselves to be in a state of divinity. Such is the case with the Swaminarayan movement, a breakaway movement within Hinduism.

Sahajanand Swami or Swaminarayan was born in the state of Uttar Pradesh in India in 1781. From about the age of 11, as was very common among spiritually inclined young men, Swaminarayan embarked on a long pilgrimage around India, in order to study yoga and the Hindu scriptures. He finally ended his seven-year pilgrimage in the state of Gujarat, where his followers expressed their conviction in his divinity. Swaminarayan was particularly well-known for his commitment concerning social and moral issues. He believed very firmly in the morality and practical value of vegetarianism, and did his best to discourage the sacrifice of animals at religious festivals. Swaminarayan did his very best to counter the unfairness and social divisiveness of the caste system. He argued that all people were equal, and that there should be no differences between the way in which men and women were treated, particularly in relation to their capacity to attain enlightenment. It was thus to be expected that the Swaminarayan movement should attract particularly members of the lower castes, since it encouraged them to see themselves as equal to others. As part of his commitment to social justice, Swaminarayan also did his best to ameliorate the conditions under which women lived in society. He argued strongly against the practice of *sati* or the custom whereby some women threw themselves on the funeral pyres of their husbands. He pointed out that in his view there was no authority in the Vedas to support this action, and that it should be discontinued.

The Swaminarayan movement is part of the bhakti tradition of Hinduism, whereby the individual concentrates on devotion to God. In parallel with this practice, the devotee attempts to shun the material pleasures of this world, and focus upon dedicating his or her life to the Divine. This approach is very similar to the philosophy enunciated in the Bhagavad Gita. The Swaminarayan movement has not been without its theological disputes and schisms. In 1906 there was, for example, a schism in the original movement. Although the breakaway movement was initially small, it later attracted many adherents and has become one of the major groups that descended from the original movement. The leader of this group is Pramukh Swami, and the history of this division is discussed in detail by Brear (1996).

A very different organization, but one in which there was again a certain degree of deification of the founder, is the Nation of Islam. The movement was founded in Detroit, in the context of the racial conflict which existed in the United States in 1930. The founder was W. D. Fard Muhammad, who was believed by the movement to be Divine. When he died in 1934, he was succeeded by one of his disciples, Elijah Muhammad. The current head of the movement is Louis Farrakhan. One of the most celebrated members of the Nation of Islam was Malcolm X. He was born Malcolm Little, but upon joining the Nation of Islam rejected his surname. It was considered within the movement that the names of black people in the United States were generally derived from their masters during the slave trade, and certainly bore no relation to their original African names. The X was thus adopted to indicate this break in the history, tradition and culture of black people, which derived from the oppression of the slave trade. Malcolm X was a very significant figure in encouraging black people to change their concept of themselves. As Saeed (2007, p. 6) argues, 'the transformation of black identity from "negro to African-American" was in large parts due to Malcolm X instilling greater self-confidence and self-esteem in the black community'. Later in his life, Malcolm X became an orthodox Muslim and adopted a Muslim name.

It is worth noting that the Nation of Islam is partly a religious movement, but also importantly an organization devoted to the achievement of social change for black people, both in the United States and worldwide. The movement is committed to the achievement of full equality for black people, and hence religious goals are combined with goals related to social justice. Elijah Muhammad outlined the key beliefs of the Nation of Islam as belief in Allah and in the Qur'an. He also argued that Allah had been personified as Fard Muhammad, which explains the general belief in the deification of the latter. Orthodox Muslims do not accept this latter claim, and indeed do not accept that the Nation of Islam is in fact an Islamic movement. They regard it on the other hand, as a religious movement which has selectively adopted some Islamic beliefs and concepts, but which cannot be thought of in any way, as truly Islamic. It is also difficult to reconcile the Nation of Islam's teachings on racism, with the traditional Islamic view that all ethnic groups can become Muslims, as all people are fundamentally equal. The idea that Fard Muhammad could bring God's direct message to human beings is impossible for orthodox Muslims to accept, since they believe that the prophet Muhammad was the 'seal of the prophets'; that is, that his revelation of God's message was the full and final revelation. Within the Nation of Islam, the teaching of Fard Muhammad has remained respected, and has continued to exert some degree of influence over members. The original leadership of new religious movements is one of the main factors in the degree of social control exerted over those who belong to the movement.

SOCIAL ORGANIZATION AND NEW RELIGIOUS MOVEMENTS

One of the criticisms made of religious movements is that considerable pressure may be exerted upon new members to conform to certain group norms. Even more so, such social pressures may, it is argued, be used to ensure conformity and indeed adherence to whatever rules or requirements are promulgated by the group leadership. In extreme cases, it is suggested, this may lead to forms of exploitation and oppression. However, an examination of a range of new religious movements suggests that this may be far from being a universal phenomenon, and that indeed new religions demonstrate a wide variety of patterns of social organization.

The Findhorn Community, for example, began life as an informal commune during the early 1960s, when there was considerable experimentation in different models of community life. It is located in Moray, on the east coast of Scotland. It began life through a series of rather serendipitous events, involving a small group of people who were interested in meditation and forms of alternative spirituality, along with various aspects of ecology and the environment. It has grown in the intervening years into a substantial ecologically based community, which has received recognition from the United Nations. The founders of the commune originally lived in caravans, but these have gradually been replaced by different types of accommodation based on 'green' principles. The Findhorn Foundation now includes a variety of community activities ranging from a publishing company, various artistic ventures and turbines for wind power. All of these activities are permeated by an informal spirituality, which also relates to the social organization of the community.

The general theory of epistemology in the movement is not one of strict adherence to a particular dogma or ideology, but of each person seeking their own way of resolving the dilemmas and questions of life. Each individual is seen as being on a personal spiritual journey, rather than following a preordained route. Admittedly, there are certain broad philosophical positions adopted within the community, for example a commitment to environmental concerns, and to certain forms of spiritual practice. However, within these very broad parameters, members embark on their own spiritual journey. The logic of this approach is that ultimately this will be a community composed of multiple perspectives. Sutcliffe (1995, p. 16) describes this phenomenon as 'the interdependency of any number of worldviews'. If this epistemological system is truly accepted then it implies a social order in which no one individual's view of the world is superior to that of any other. It is a social order in which all agree to accept diversity.

STUDY QUESTION

Such a micro-society does require some type of social 'cement' to bind it together, for otherwise there is the continual risk of fragmentation, as everyone may think that their view of the world is the correct one. If each person considers their perception of the world to be valid, then it requires considerable qualities of tolerance within the community to ensure that there is a minimum of tension and friction. On the other hand, such a philosophy can also be conducive to genuine democratic freedoms, as people learn to accept that no one can legitimately try to control the group and assume power. Everyone must be permitted to have a say in the governance of the group.

To what extent can a new religious movement retain a sense of cohesion, if members hold a range of spiritual views?

Some new religious movements seem to be able to combine a clear sense of leadership and centralized direction, with an overall sense of democracy and equality of human beings. Such is the case of the Baha'i faith, whose origin is normally considered to have occurred with the teachings of Siyyid Ali-Muhammad who came from Shiraz in Persia, and who assumed the name of the 'Bap'. He regarded himself as a messiah of God. The teachings of the Bap brought him into conflict with the prevalent Muslim hierarchy in Persia and as a result he was executed in 1850. One of his disciples was a man named Mirza Husayn Ali Nuri who assumed the name Baha'u'llah. He continued the tradition of the Bap's teachings, but after a period of imprisonment was banished from Iran, residing subsequently in a series of countries. During this period those who were committed to the teachings of the Bap started to give their loyalty to Baha'u'llah, and the latter began to speak of the religious movement as the Baha'i movement. Baha'u'llah died in what is now Israel in 1892. He was succeeded by his son Abbas Effendi who became known as Abdul-Baha, and subsequently by Abdul-Baha's grandson Shoghi Effendi. The latter died in 1957. After Shoghi Effendi the direction and leadership of the movement was taken over by the 'Universal House of Justice', a democratically elected body, membership of which is for a five-year term.

Some of the principles of the Baha'i faith lead to particular forms of social interaction within the Baha'i community. Central to Baha'i philosophy is the concept of the unity of all human beings. This is not to argue that all human beings are equal in the sense of being identical, but rather that they are equal in all possessing the same rights and dignities as human beings. In addition, as all human beings are perceived as the creation of one God, then there is the concept of all human beings being interrelated. This also gives all of us a sense of responsibility towards all other human beings. Chin (2006, p. 31) in a study of a sample of Baha'i women in the United States notes that 'in the absence of a collective consciousness and recognition of the world's peoples as one common family, there can be no equitable and authentic changes to the world's many and wide-ranging social, economic and political problems'.

This notion of the basic equality of human beings tends to reduce the possibility of discrimination within the Baha'i community. Just as there is the concept of equality between human beings, Baha'is also have respect for the equality of different faiths. They regard different religions as having been revealed by the same one God, and hence having the same basic religious and spiritual beliefs in common. Although individual religions clearly have differences in ritual, scripture and practice, these are regarded as a corollary of the cultural and social circumstances which existed at the time that a religion came into being. The Baha'i position on the nature of spiritual revelation is that religions will continue to be revealed, with each new faith providing insights which are particularly relevant to the new social situation. Overall such a world view tends to create a social system where there is respect for others, tolerance of a diversity of views and a reluctance to adopt an egocentric approach.

The Baha'i faith developed in an Islamic society and although it found itself in considerable conflict with Islam, it gradually expanded to become a global movement which attracted people from a variety of different world views and cultures. The Ahmadiyya movement also developed in a Muslim context, starting in the town of Qadian in what is now the Indian part of Punjab. The movement was founded by Mirza Ghulam Ahmad in 1889. He saw himself as the *Mahdi*, the arrival of whom was anticipated by Muslims. In addition, he perceived the movement as helping Islam to return to a former purity which had been allegedly lost or abandoned over the centuries since its foundation. Neither of these claims endeared the Ahmadis to the surrounding Muslim majority. But there were other contentious areas. The concept of *jihad* requires Muslims to struggle against any immoral or unethical tendencies, and to aspire to the best possible conduct. This is accepted generally by all orthodox Muslims and also by Ahmadis. However, orthodox Muslims also argue that if Islam is physically or ideologically attacked in any way, the principle of jihad requires all Muslims to go to its defence. Ahmadis, however, generally adopt a different view. They do not feel that violence should be met with violence, but that wherever possible a peaceful solution should be found. The other principal area of contention is that orthodox Muslims believe very firmly and absolutely that the prophet Muhammad was the 'seal of the prophets' and that no prophet would come after him. Some Ahmadis consider that Mirza Ghulam Ahmed was merely someone who reformed Islam rather than being an actual prophet. Other Ahmadis, however, believe that there is a possibility for further prophets after Muhammad, although they will not be as great. This ambiguity within the Ahmadiyya movement about the status of the prophet Muhammad has caused great strength of feeling among orthodox Muslims, and often intense antipathy towards Ahmadis. This has sometimes taken the form of persecution, attacks on the community and a considerable number of deaths. Nevertheless the movement continues to expand throughout the world, particularly in the West. Their position with regard to Muslim orthodoxy remains at the centre of two entirely different perspectives. The Ahmadis consider themselves to be quite clearly Muslims, while orthodox Islam regards them as a totally separate faith which is definitely not Muslim. Mainstream Muslims would not then regard them as a sect of Islam, to use the terminology of the previous chapter. The persistent persecution which they have faced has probably resulted in a strong sense of communal cohesion within the movement, and a determination to survive. This perhaps also explains the determined trend towards proselytization which can be observed. If the movement is to survive the antagonism towards it, then it must surely feel the need to continue to grow in numbers.

One of the features of new religious movements is that they are frequently a challenge in some way to existing religions, and that this process of challenge has consequences for the social organization of the movement. Conversely, the social organization of a new movement can also sometimes constitute a challenge. For example, in the early days of the development of Pentecostalism in the first decade of the twentieth century in California, it was very much a multiethnic movement, at a time when there was very strict racial segregation throughout most of American society. In addition the forms which religious practice took in the Pentecostal movement resulted in a good deal of consternation among other Christian denominations.

Pentecostalism is a relatively new movement within Christianity which tries to recapture the types of spiritual experience which were apparently evident during the early years of the Christian Church. Indeed it argues that such forms of spirituality exist nowadays and people need only avail themselves of them. These forms of spirituality include faith healing, the existence of miracles and prophecies, and what is usually described as 'speaking in tongues'. The latter is the phenomenon of a person speaking in an apparently unknown language during a religious gathering, and perhaps through this passing on a spiritual message. This message may require interpretation. The appearance of the ability to speak in tongues is usually assumed to be evidence that the person concerned has been affected by the spirit of God. It is interesting that Pentecostalism has often developed in areas of relative poverty and social deprivation, particularly where faith healing was a great attraction. It is difficult to determine whether people in such areas were attracted to faith healing because it was an inexpensive form of health care, or because of its spiritual content. Certainly, Avalos (2001, p. 3) in a study of Pentecostalism in the southern United States and Mexico argues that 'many new religious traditions begin as alternative health care systems, or promote alternative health care as a main component'.

Although some of the features of contemporary Pentecostalism have no doubt arisen spontaneously over the years in different congregations, the movement is generally dated from religious meetings which took place in a meeting house on Azusa Street, Los Angeles in 1906. The services were led by William J. Seymour, who was African

33

American in origin. The congregation consisted typically of people of many different ethnic groups and social backgrounds. The meetings were very informal. If members of the congregation felt the presence of God, they might call out or walk to the front of the meeting hall to make a statement. From the very beginning women were also encouraged to assume leadership roles in the church. The 'revival' as it was called lasted about ten years at Azusa Street and then started to decline there. However, it had acted as a catalyst for Pentecostalism which began to spread throughout the world.

Pentecostal communities and congregations were often characterized by a focus on the 'second coming' of Jesus Christ, and by the claim that people would 'prophesy' before that event. There was an emphasis upon non-violence, and Pentecostals generally did not participate in warfare, normally declaring themselves to be conscientious objectors. Pentecostals could be characterized as a sect, if we chose to use that concept, since the movement represents a separation from the main stock of Christianity. Quite apart from its spiritual practices, its sense of equality in terms of race and gender and its opposition to violence have often placed the movement in clear opposition to other denominations and congregations.

There is no strong central direction to the movement, and there is considerable diversity within Pentecostalism. Indeed some of its variants or practices may be viewed as extreme. An example would be the handling of poisonous snakes, which is an element in many of the Pentecostal Church services in the Appalachian mountains of Kentucky and West Virginia in the United States. Although there is some apparent Biblical basis for the snake handling, it is difficult to establish whether the practice is spiritual in origin or has a more prosaic social basis. It has been noted for example (see Tidball and Tourney, 2007) that as large mining companies persuaded Appalachian mountain residents to sign away mineral rights, the latter sought a means of retaining a pride in their culture. This then resulted in their developing the practice of serpent handling. Tidball and Tourney (2007, p. 8) suggest that 'serpent-handling rituals arose as a result of capitalism reducing Appalachian people to a rural proletariat dispossessed from its lands . . .'

One might therefore argue that phenomena such as serpent-handling, while appearing eccentric and indeed antagonistic to more established religious belief, may serve a more positive social function. It may help the small communities of the Appalachian

Mountains in preserving a feeling of solidarity and social cohesion. Although new religious movements, perhaps by their very 'newness', may be challenging for established religion, that challenge need not be a negative factor, but may help religion adapt to changing social situations.

FURTHER READING

Barrett, D. V. (2001) *The New Believers: Sects, 'Cults', and Alternative Religions*, London: Cassell.
Clarke, P. B. (2006) *New Religions in Global Perspective: A Study of Religious Change in the Modern World*, London: Routledge.
McGrath, A. (ed.) (1995) *Blackwell Encyclopedia of Modern Christian Thought*, Oxford: Blackwell.
Partridge, C. (ed.) (2003) *UFO Religions*, London: Routledge.
Wallis, R. (1984) *The Elementary Forms of New Religious Life*, London: Routledge and Kegan Paul.

PART II

A SURVEY OF NEW RELIGIOUS MOVEMENTS

CHAPTER 3

MOVEMENTS RELATED TO HINDUISM

This chapter discusses five different new religious movements which have evolved from the Hindu religious tradition. In the decades following the Second World War, the growing youth counterculture developed a close empathy with the philosophical and religious traditions of India. Many Hindu teachers achieved celebrity status in the West, and the movements which they founded developed rapidly. This chapter examines some movements, which in different ways reflected the spirit of the period.

ANANDA MARGA

Establishment

Ananda Marga is a spiritual and philosophical new religious movement, which also has a substantial history of contributing to social development in different parts of the world. It was founded in India in 1955.

The founder of the movement was Prabhat Ranjan Sarkar who was also known by his religious name of Shrii Shrii Anandamurti. He was born in 1921 in the state of Bihar in eastern India. As a young man he studied at the University of Calcutta and was clearly a very able student. During the rest of his life he demonstrated considerable academic ability in a range of fields from religious philosophy to social theory, and as an author. After university he worked for Indian railways as an accountant, but continued with his interests in religious and social development. During this period he started to teach meditation and traditional Indian spirituality to friends and acquaintances, and gradually began to acquire a reputation as a religious teacher. By 1955 the time seemed appropriate to start a formal organization built around the principles which he taught, and so he initiated the Ananda Marga organization, or Path of Bliss. He continued to work as an accountant in order to support his extended family, but the Ananda Marga gradually expanded. Sarkar started to put many of his ideas on Indian religion into writing, and began what would be an extensive career as an author. Seven years after the foundation of the movement, he established first an order of monks, and later an order of nuns. From 1966 onwards he gave up his employment with Indian railways, and worked full-time for the organization he had founded. Centres were gradually established in different countries as the reputation of Ananda Marga spread.

From the early 1970s onwards some of Sarkar's philosophy and teaching brought him into conflict with the Indian government and local state government. As a result of various charges made against him, he was imprisoned. As a protest against what he regarded as false charges he commenced a fast in 1973 consuming only a small quantity of milk every day. He maintained this fast until 1978 when he was eventually released.

In 1979 he embarked on a journey to visit many of the Ananda Marga centres overseas, and to give his personal support to their work. He continued to establish trusts and charitable organizations associated with Ananda Marga, including a university in West Bengal. Sarkar died on 21 October 1990.

Teachings

The overall teaching of Ananda Marga may be summarized as the development and perfection of the individual, coupled with a parallel development of the universe as a whole. The Ananda Marga approach to personal development involves a variety of methods including meditation, hatha yoga, dietary practices, and a devotion to helping the less-fortunate members of society. The organization also places great emphasis upon providing opportunities for education and for health care. For example, the yoga teachings of Ananda Marga were part of a study of how yoga might enhance a national health service (Siegel and de Barros, 2009, p. 97). It is thus an integrated system of development which attempts to combine personal spiritual enhancement with an ethical response to the external world.

Sarkar's theology was monotheistic, with the idea of a God who is the creator of the universe, and who cares for all beings. The responsibility of each human being is to offer love for God and to devote his or her life to this devotion. Hence it would not be philosophically sufficient to devote one's life to the spiritual perfection of oneself since this would be to ignore a large proportion of God's creation. This is therefore the basis of the idea of social service and responsibility for others which is at the heart of Ananda Marga.

In terms of personal development, the organization recommends the use of meditation. As with most forms of meditation there is an attempt to focus and concentrate the mind, rather than allowing random thoughts to occupy it. The particular focus in Ananda Marga is to concentrate on the feelings of bliss which derive from devotion to God. A mantram is widely used as a technique to achieve this. Within the Ananda Marga organization, a member will be taught meditation by an experienced teacher who will guide their progress. The system of meditation used is sometimes termed sahaj yoga, which implies a yoga dedicated to a sense of union with God. Sarkar also referred to his system as a branch of tantra, devoted to the freeing of the spirit. Tantra yoga perceives the mind as frequently ensnared within a network of negative ideas and systems of thought acquired during one's life. The individual who studies meditation systematically is seen as being able to gradually escape from these acquired systems of thought, and attain a sense of calmness and serenity.

Sarkar argues that tantra has often been seen as a rather subjective and egoistic pursuit of personal fulfilment and realization. To achieve such ends, tantric practitioners have often employed a variety of techniques of an extreme type which have given tantra a less than positive reputation. However, the genuine tantra is seen within Ananda Marga as a spiritual strategy which is directed from the individual towards the external world, in order to benefit others.

As with most systems of yoga, Sarkar recommends the daily practice of yoga postures or asanas, and the use of breathing exercises or pranayama. In addition, students of tantra yoga are advised to adopt a vegetarian diet. The ultimate purpose of such yoga practice is union with God. It is considered impossible to conceive of God, since human mental faculties are inadequate to grasp the scale of the Divine. Nevertheless, God is perceived as having revealed a part of himself in the phenomenal universe. Although the latter exhibits

41

all the limitations and inadequacies of the physical world, it is still the responsibility of human beings to work for this world, as it is a manifestation of God.

Social organization

Ananda Marga is a highly structured worldwide organization, which in terms of administration is divided into a number of geographical divisions. Within the overall organization, there are different departments with specific aims. There is a department devoted to worldwide relief efforts in the event of natural disasters and famine. The organization also provides extensive medical care in underdeveloped parts of the world. There are also departments devoted to education and to women's equality and opportunity issues.

One of the main educational developments was the foundation of the Ananda Marga University in India. This is linked to a worldwide network of schools and institutions. Notably, Ananda Marga has been active in rural development and in establishing schools in village communities where otherwise educational opportunities for children would have been very limited. The organization has also established many centres for the teaching of yoga and meditation. Every agency or institution developed within the organization tends to be structured in keeping with the main principle of Ananda Marga which is a combination of individual, internal spiritual development, linked to a sense of service to the community at large.

Ethical issues

The ethical perspective of Ananda Marga is rooted in the concept of a God who has created the universe and all animate and inanimate forms within it. The fact that we are all linked by this single creation gives us a sense of moral responsibility towards all living things. From this also stems a sense of equality with all beings, and hence feelings of superiority are dispelled whether based upon gender, race, nationality or any other criterion. Sarkar had reservations about the way in which the capitalist system of economics functioned in society since he felt that it reinforced inequalities rather than helping to spread equality among human beings.

Sarkar encapsulated his philosophy in the concept of neohumanism. This approach encourages people to have a philosophy of life which is all-embracing, including a sense of the need to support the environment, to support the less-wealthy and disadvantaged, to provide an education system which espoused such values, and to develop an economic system which distributed wealth fairly. He argued against the trend towards a materialistic society and encouraged a society based upon genuine love and respect for fellow human beings.

This philosophy of a fairer economic system was defined in Sarkar's Progressive Utilization Theory. In this he sought to argue that no existing economic system had proved satisfactory for the world, and what was needed was a new system based upon spiritual neohumanism. In short, such a new economic system must be based upon a genuine egalitarian distribution of wealth.

Sarkar also proposed spiritual theories of existence, which while incapable of being definitely verified by empirical science appear to explain aspects of the human condition. He proposed that small particles of energy, microvita, were produced in negative and positive forms in living beings. If a person did not lead a balanced, spiritual life then negative microvita were formed which ultimately could lead to illness. On the other hand, a life led according to neohumanist principles encouraged the development of positive microvita, which were conducive to a healthy, disease-free existence.

STUDY QUESTION

Sarkar's view of human progress is that we should not seek our own pleasure, success or advancement at the expense of others. To do so would be contrary to his concept of universal responsibility. Individuals should always consider the consequences of their actions for the living world, the inorganic world and the universe in general. In this way we preserve the equilibrium of the world around us.

Are there similarities here with ethical systems in other religions, such as for example, 'non-attachment' in Buddhism?

Overall it is difficult to fault the principles of P. R. Sarkar, and many of these, for example, in the spheres of ecology and environmentalism, have become part of mainstream thought. As a large and complex organization it is no doubt often difficult to ensure that neohumanist principles are adhered to consistently, although the principles themselves appear very laudatory.

DIVINE LIGHT MISSION

Establishment

The roots of this Hindu movement devoted to self-realization may be traced back to the north Indian teacher Shri Hans Maharaj Ji who was active between the 1930s and the 1960s. Starting as an individual teacher, he gradually developed a following and in 1960 established the Divine Light Mission in order to spread his teaching. Shri Hans Maharaj Ji died in 1966, and by that time his philosophical approach had spread very widely in India, and members numbered over a million.

There was some debate about who would succeed the founder, but eventually it was agreed that his youngest son Prem Rawat would become the spiritual leader of the organization. As he was 8 years of age, there was, perhaps understandably, some discussion about whether his leadership would be appropriate, but he found considerable support within the organization. However, he was unable to assume any legal authority for the Divine Light Mission, and different members of his family had to take responsibility for this. Five years after becoming the spiritual leader, Prem Rawat travelled to the United States and England in order to expand the Divine Light Mission and to start ashrams. He was very successful in this, and in the United States the Mission was accepted as a religious body for taxation purposes. The organization managed to establish bases in a number of different countries, and also to found movements in the area of health care and social provision.

During the early 1970s the Divine Light Mission was probably viewed in the public consciousness as being part of the broad counterculture movement, although it may in fact have had a rather more serious-minded strand to its thought and activities than may be assumed by this generalization. Nevertheless, spiritual festivals were a significant element during this period. Members of the Divine Light Mission paid to attend, and this raised significant amounts of money. Major festivals were held in India, England and the United States during the early 1970s. However, there was evidence that the organization owed considerable amounts of money at this period, and members participated in various money-raising ventures. By the mid-1970s Prem Rawat started to restructure the Divine Light Mission, slowly removing much of the terminology, ritual and beliefs which defined its origin as being basically Hindu. He appears to have wanted to appeal to a broader cultural audience who did not necessarily want an Indian-oriented organization but preferred one which was concerned with self-realization within a non-specific cultural context.

At the same time that he was planning these changes, Prem Rawat married. Perhaps the fact that he married an American, rather than someone of Indian ethnicity, was at least partly responsible for the dissent which occurred in his family and in the management of the organization. In 1975 the organization in India came under the control of Prem Rawat's mother, while Rawat himself assumed control of the Mission in the remainder of the world.

In 1983, following a legal process, the name of the Divine Light Mission was changed to Elan Vital, to reflect the transition from a Hindu-oriented organization. Elan Vital itself is in the process of changing to organizations named 'Words of Peace International' and 'Words of Peace Global'. At about the time of the transition to Elan Vital, Rawat became known as Maharaji.

Teachings

Prem Rawat's father, Hans Ji Maharaj was a guru in his own right, and was known in particular for the way in which he brought religious teaching to poorer people. He was not preoccupied with the caste of those he taught, nor with whether his disciples were Hindu or Muslim. In a country with very sharp cultural divisions between these religions, this was unusual.

Prem Rawat inherited the same philosophy of religious teaching as his father, taking a broadly non-dogmatic and non-doctrinaire approach. In terms of placing him within a particular school of thought, Prem Rawat is often considered as being part of the so-called Sant tradition of northern India. The sants or saints were an informal network of spiritual teachers who were devoted to God, but not by means of external practice. Geaves (2009, p. 24), for example, argues that 'in the Indian context, both Prem Rawat and his father denied the possibility of the use of rituals or outer forms of religion to access the inner divine.' The sants generally taught using local dialects and colloquial forms of language, in order to communicate with farmers and villagers. They did not all espouse an identical teaching, but reflected these broad approaches.

> **STUDY QUESTION**
>
> The Sant tradition also had a great influence upon Guru Nanak, the founder of the Sikh religion. Indeed when the holy scripture of the Sikhs, the Guru Granth Sahib, was compiled, the writings of a number of Sants including Kabir, Namdev and Sheikh Farid were included.
>
> Perhaps the Sant tradition suggests a trend in Indian religiosity which is more integrative and less concerned with distinctions between faiths. What do you think about this?

Prem Rawat is also considered part of the *bhakti* or devotional school of Hinduism, which is concerned with focusing internally to find God, rather than looking externally. This is partly achieved through the use of four types of meditation which Rawat calls the 'Knowledge'. Prem Rawat's 'Knowledge' is very practical in approach, rather than, for example, using extensive prayers and scripture. He has tended therefore not to synthesize a body of religious knowledge which can be taught in a fairly rigid manner. He is flexible in his teaching tending to change his approach and organizational structure in order to meet the needs of new developments in society. Nor does he appear to be rigid or very prescriptive in terms of the extent to which disciples adhere to his teachings. People are encouraged to try to practise his system of spiritual self-development, but not necessarily to continue if it does not appear to generate satisfactory results. Prem Rawat has not tended to use complex concepts as part of his religious thinking, preferring instead to encourage his followers to employ the practical meditation strategies of the 'Knowledge'. The techniques do not appear to be perceived as an element of a religion per se, but perhaps rather as part of a spiritual system which encourages people towards a state of fulfilment and self-realization. In addition, Prem Rawat has generally not seemed to adopt a highly directive role, but to present his teachings to people for them to try to evaluate if they so wish.

Social organization

There are a number of features of the overall philosophy of the Divine Light Mission which suggest a relatively democratic approach to social organization, and a non-authoritarian leadership style. The separation of the organization from the Hindu tradition, and the embracing of a more generalized spirituality, tends to minimize the possibility of strict adherence to certain rituals or scriptural texts. In turn this encourages a less rigid approach to spiritual practice. There also seems to have been an encouragement for members to live ordinary lives of working in employment or being involved in charitable work, rather than asceticism. It could be argued that the latter encourages a degree of extremism in religious practice which may be less present when people are leading more conventional lives. Prem Rawat appears to draw upon teachings from a range of religions which gives a sense of eclecticism to the movement. In addition, by not seeking to transmit a specific, or indeed dogmatic, range of teaching, it permits followers a certain degree of freedom of thought and the capacity to make sense of religious experience in their own way.

Ethical issues

Prem Rawat appears to have inherited from his father as well as from the Sant tradition, a sense of the equality of all men and women. This important ethical principle contrasts somewhat with the social and religious hierarchy of the caste system in India, and also with the male domination which is generally found in most religious systems including Hinduism. It does not appear that people are asked to pay specifically for the meditation teachings of Prem Rawat, although generally disciples may be invited to contribute to the upkeep of the organization. The funding of new religious movements is a delicate matter with ethical implications. Generally, it could be argued that religious knowledge is qualitatively different from most other knowledge. We may be willing to pay someone to show us how to repair our car, but we may feel that religious knowledge should be given freely. On the other hand, we may differentiate between say paying for meditation advice, and helping to pay for the infrastructure of a religious organization.

From its inception, the Divine Light Mission was not exclusively concerned with spiritual self-fulfilment, but helped to establish health centres and organizations devoted to disadvantaged members of society. This type of involvement almost certainly helps to develop a sound public reputation for a new religious movement which might otherwise be thought of as introverted and introspective in its approach.

INTERNATIONAL SOCIETY FOR KRISHNA
CONSCIOUSNESS (ISKCON)

Establishment

The International Society for Krishna Consciousness (ISKCON) was founded in 1966 by a Hindu spiritual teacher, A. C. Bhaktivedanta Swami Prabhupada. This new religious movement is frequently referred to as the Hare Krishna Movement, partly at least with reference to the mantram which is chanted by members. Prabhupada was born in 1896 and died in 1977. His home town was Calcutta, and his original name as a child was Abhay Charan. He received a formal education at a British school in Calcutta, studying both Indian and Western culture.

ISKCON was not simply started in 1966 without any preparation. In fact, Prabhupada had been involved in spiritual teaching and writing since the 1930s. His own personal guru was Bhaktisiddhanta Sarasvati Thakura who had encouraged him to disseminate the teachings which he had learned. In the early 1940s he established a religious magazine entitled 'Back to Godhead'. He later lived in a monastery which had an extensive library of Sanskrit texts, and he began translating them for a contemporary readership. This was the beginning of the major publishing enterprise which would be a feature of ISKCON for years to come. In 1959 he became a swami, and six years later he travelled to the United States with the specific intention of establishing ISKCON. The latter was founded in New York in 1966, in a premises which served as a temple. During the following year another temple was founded in San Francisco. This was a period during which there was an intense interest in Indian culture among young people, and ISKCON expanded rapidly throughout North America. Members of the movement also travelled to London where branches of ISKCON were established. In 1971 Prabhupada travelled back to India, in order partly to support the establishment of a series of ISKCON temples. This movement underwent a dramatically rapid expansion, in the United States and Europe during the 1960s and early 1970s. The so-called youth counterculture was in full flow at the time, and Hindu culture was an integral element of this. It made its appearance in art, clothing, design and music, while the intrinsic tolerance and relativism of Hindu philosophy linked well with the sense of freedom and liberalism of the times. The interest expressed by the Beatles and particularly George Harrison, in Hinduism, did much to extend interest in ISKCON.

Teachings

The teaching of ISKCON rests within the bhakti or devotional tradition of Hinduism, which in this case manifests itself as devotion to Krishna, as a reflection of the absolute God. Within this tradition there is also the custom of attaching great devotion to a personal guru who passes on spiritual learning to a disciple. Bhakti is found in many different schools of religious thought in India, but in terms of devotion to the God Vishnu of whom Krishna is a personification, it first came to prominence among a group of southern Indian saints called the Alvars. From about the ninth century onwards they were a key factor in disseminating the idea of devotion to Vishnu. Bhakti, as a religious philosophy, became one of the most influential movements in Hinduism.

The scripture perhaps most commonly associated with bhakti is the Bhagavad Gita, and this became central to the religious life of ISKCON members. The Bhagavad Gita is set just before a major battle between two armies; many of the soldiers in one army being related to those in the other. On one side Prince Arjuna has Lord Krishna as his charioteer. Before the battle commences, Arjuna begins to have considerable reservations about fighting, as he knows he has many family relatives in the opposing army. He confides in Krishna and the latter uses this opportunity to outline to Arjuna a range of philosophical and spiritual advice in order to help him both resolve his internal conflicts and also lead his life in an ethical manner.

STUDY QUESTION

The Gita was apparently the favourite scriptural text of Mahatma Gandhi. He reputedly carried a copy of it when he was imprisoned by the British during the campaign for Indian freedom. Gandhi used it as a source of inspiration during these times. Chapter 2 of the Gita appears to have been his favourite chapter.

Try reading the last 18 verses of chapter 2 of the Gita. Why do you think it inspired Gandhi?

A considerable part of the Bhagavad Gita is a discourse on the nature of Bhakti yoga. Krishna says that all human beings should devote their lives to Him, including the deeds that they perform, and in so doing, they will escape from the cycle of birth, death and transmigration, gaining *moksha* or release.

Prabhupada set out to disseminate spiritual teaching and in particular to pass on the teaching associated with the worship of Krishna. A central part of this was the publishing and marketing of a variety of books all connected with the worship of Krishna, and some written by Prabhupada. The publication system of ISKCON is part of their extensive education system, but also a reflection of their notion of teaching passing in succession from guru to disciple and then onwards.

One of the most significant aspects of ISKCON is the teaching regarding the repetition of the mantram, Hare Krishna Hare Krishna, Krishna Krishna Hare Hare, Hare Rama Hare Rama, Rama Rama Hare Hare. Chanting or repetition of this is said to bring about a deep spiritual awareness of God.

Prabhupada established the Bhaktivedanta Book Trust in 1972 under whose auspices were published many of his translations and commentaries upon Sanskrit religious texts, including on the Bhagavad Gita. Prabhupada held a tolerant and relativistic view towards other faiths, believing that all the world's main religions were fundamentally a manifestation of the same religious spirit.

Social organization

ISKCON was established by Prabhupada as a well-organized movement with what could perhaps best be described as a stratified rather than hierarchical structure. Networks of temples were established around the world, with one of the most famous ones being at Vrindavan where Krishna is said to have lived.

The Governing Body Commission is the main management commission of ISKCON with responsibility for general organizational and policy decisions of the movement. ISKCON has sub-organizations, one devoted to the distribution of food aid around the world in places of need, and another dedicated to passing on their teachings to young people. ISKCON has approximately 50 schools around the world, including a primary school at Bhaktivedanta Manor in Hertfordshire, England.

Ethical issues

The approach to other religions mentioned above suggests a tolerant, non-dogmatic view within this movement. Rules and regulations appear to be relatively minimal. In terms of food, the movement is vegetarian, which probably reflects the ancient Hindu tradition of ahimsa, or non-violence. In relation to ethics, it sets itself against the use of drugs, and supports basic interpersonal moral values.

SAI BABA MOVEMENT

Establishment

This new religious movement was founded by a Hindu teacher, Sathya Sai Baba. The movement developed gradually during the 1960s and 1970s. Sai Baba's name at birth was Sathyanarayana Raju, and he was born in the state of Andhra Pradesh, in India in 1926. When he was 14 he experienced something of a medical crisis, and during this he declared that he was a reincarnation of a Hindu holy man who had died in the early years of the twentieth century. That spiritual leader was Sai Baba of Shirdi.

In his life, Shirdi Sai Baba was a very celebrated teacher and guru, who was well-known, among other things, for his custom of trying to synthesize Hindu and Muslim ideas. It is unclear where he was actually born, and indeed whether he was born as a Muslim or Hindu. In reality he appeared to combine many of the characteristics, both in his teaching and in customs, of a Sufi as well as a Hindu guru. As is suggested by his name, he spent a good deal of his life in the village of Shirdi, in the state of Maharashtra. At the time this was a small village, predominantly devoted to agriculture, and with a largely Hindu population, along with a small but significant Muslim minority (Srinivas, 1999, p. 90). He lived the life of an ascetic, offering healing to those who were ill and caring for visitors and travellers whether they were Hindu or Muslim.

In his teachings, Shirdi Sai Baba appeared to have a great deal in common with the Bhakti tradition. He encouraged people to devote themselves to God rather than to material possessions, and he also considered that God was one, whether worshipped by Muslims, Christians or Hindus. He advocated a simple life of faith, caring for others, and doing his best to provide food and water to those who needed it. Towards the end of his life, he became well-known throughout India, as disciples spread his message.

It is impossible to pass judgement upon whether there is any truth in the claim of reincarnation. One can say that there are some similarities between the teachings of Shirdi Sai Baba and those of Sathya Sai Baba, although this of course provides no evidence of reincarnation. When Sathya Sai Baba was 24 years of age, he completed the building of an ashram in the village of his birth, and four years later he added a hospital. He continued to develop medical and health projects throughout his life, building ashrams and hospitals.

Teachings

The Sai Baba movement has a fairly eclectic set of teachings which do not appear to have been synthesized into a specific belief system. Many of the teachings of Sai Baba would probably be recognized as acceptable and valid within the broad spectrum of Hindu religious practice. Sathya Sai Baba was teaching a monotheism that accepts the concept of God in other religions, and indeed felt that all faiths point to the same, single God of the universe. As part of the regular spiritual practice of the movement, members sing hymns and meditate.

Throughout his life, Sai Baba had arranged meetings with his disciples wherever possible, in order to teach and advise them. On these occasions and at other times he had been observed producing jewellery, and a variety of other objects, as if out of nowhere. Some have seen such events as examples of his miraculous powers, while others view them as fraudulent tricks designed to impress people. In the absence of conclusive evidence in either direction, it seems appropriate to suspend judgement.

Sai Baba had emphasized in his teachings that all human beings should aspire to recognize the spirituality within themselves. In other words we should all realize that in principle we possess some divine qualities within us, and that it behoves us to try to live according to these qualities. Sai Baba did not tend to convert this general idea into specific injunctions for members of his organization. His teachings tended to be maintained on the level of general religious and moral principles. He did, however, emphasize spiritual ideas which would be recognized in many other Hindu traditions. Ahimsa or non-violence was emphasized, along with the principle of behaving towards other human beings in a peaceful way. Meditation is practised extensively, along with the repetition of the name of God.

STUDY QUESTION

Chanting the name of God, either aloud, or repeating it silently, is a common form of meditation in the Indian religious tradition. It is an important part, for example, of the Sikh religious practice. The name of God acts, in effect, as a form of mantram, and the steady repetition helps to calm the mind, and make it receptive for more advanced meditational activities.

What other forms of mantra are used in Indian meditation?

Social organization

The Sai Baba organization exists on a worldwide basis, with a network of ashrams, hospitals and other centres devoted to charitable works. It has a fairly complex hierarchical system in terms of its management. This may well be necessary in terms of maintaining effective administrative control over a complex organization, but there is the danger that it would provide unanticipated barriers between ordinary members and the spiritual leadership of the movement. Health care is a major concern of the movement, with specific centres having been established for the amelioration of leprosy and to help with the development of health care infrastructure in rural areas. Sathya Sai Baba was a popular Hindu religious figure, and even among people who are not members of the movement, he may still be venerated (Shah, 2006, p. 211).

Ethical issues

Much of the work of the organization is underpinned by moral principles. Sai Baba has argued that it was not his intention to create a movement which had himself at the head, as an object of personal devotion. He has argued that his ambition was to disseminate the kind of spiritual teachings in which he believed, and which he thought could help people live better lives. He has also argued that he did not specifically intend to recruit large numbers of disciples or to create a very large organization. Nevertheless, many of these have in effect occurred, albeit without any deliberate intent, and this does no doubt create problems in how to manage such an organization.

Although he placed great emphasis upon participating in social projects which would help humanity, Sai Baba was also very keen that this should not be done with a view to gaining any kind of reward. In particular those who gave of their time, money or energy should not hope or expect to receive anything from those who are helped. This he felt was an important moral principle.

THE RAJNEESH/OSHO ORGANIZATION

Establishment

The founder of the Rajneesh movement was born in 1931 and named Rajneesh Chandra Mohan. His parents were members of the Jain religion and he was born in the village of Kuchwara in the state of Madhya Pradesh. At school it quickly became evident that he was very able intellectually, and particularly good in oral discussion. However, he sometimes expressed his views in such a way that he irritated and alienated his teachers. He studied philosophy for his Bachelor of Arts degree which he obtained in 1955, and this was followed two years later by a Master of Arts in philosophy from the University of Sagar. In 1958 he obtained a post as a philosophy lecturer at the University of Jabalpur.

STUDY QUESTION

Although Rajneesh later gained something of a reputation as an unorthodox, unpredictable and even somewhat irrational teacher, it is important to remember that he had a strong academic education in both Western and Eastern philosophy. This later enabled him, in both his writing and oral discourses, to appeal to an international audience.

Can you research other Indian teachers who successfully integrated Western and Indian traditions?

While lecturing at the university he started to give talks on spiritual matters, to run meditation sessions, and gradually to develop a reputation as a religious teacher and guru. People consulted him for advice on spiritual matters, and he became more and more known as a spiritual teacher. He was already something of an iconoclast, criticizing many aspects of orthodox Hinduism, and challenging the authority of established Hindu leaders. In many ways he was a modernist, with a contemporary vision of India, which included the idea of industrial expansion linked to a liberal economy, with a reduced emphasis on traditional religious protocols. He was also critical of social norms and values which were largely founded upon religious mores and culture, and in particular he advocated a far more liberal approach to sexual relations between people. This was highly contentious in the India of the time, but while attracting criticism, it also brought publicity and some supporting advocates.

The help of wealthy supporters and disciples enabled Rajneesh to establish an ashram in Pune, one of the major cities of the state of Maharashtra. From the mid-1970s onwards this ashram expanded, offering meditation and therapy sessions, and a variety of related sales outlets. Gradually more and more Western young people heard of the ashram and came to stay in Pune. However, Rajneesh's teaching style and some of the group activities in the ashram were ever-controversial. Even the national government became concerned about the reputation of the ashram, and the latter was placed under more and more scrutiny. In 1981 Rajneesh decided to visit the United States, and one of the results of this trip was the purchase of a large ranch in the state of Oregon, which was to serve as a new Rajneesh ashram. The ranch was surrounded by rural, farming land and small farming communities. It is probably not surprising that there developed conflict between the rapidly growing ashram community and the indigenous residents. From 1981 onwards it became the aspiration of the ashram community to found a 'town' on the ranch, which had all the kind of urban facilities and services normally associated with an urban development. This indeed came into being, and Rajneesh himself lived in the 'town'. The organization was very successful at developing income-generating strategies, and established a number of commercial organizations both in the US and abroad.

In 1985 Rajneesh was accused of making false statements to the United States immigration authorities when he first applied to visit the country. He was subsequently arrested and eventually pleaded guilty without the case having to go to court. As a result he agreed to leave the United States. Then followed a period when he flew to a number of countries, all of whom refused him entry or a residence permit. He eventually returned to the ashram in Pune in 1986. By now he was having health problems, but continued to do some limited teaching and meditation instruction. In 1989 he changed his name to Osho. He died in 1990 at the age of 58 years. His life was extremely eventful and complex, and as D'Andrea (2007, p. 96) suggests, 'a detailed and objective biography is yet to be written . . .'.

Teachings

One of the interesting aspects of Rajneesh was his personal qualities as a teacher. He appears to have possessed considerable charisma, and to have had a great influence on those who were in his presence. He did not necessarily present his teachings in a logical manner in the style of Western rationalism, but appeared on many occasions to be deliberately irrational, trying to challenge and to shock his listeners. In this, he had something in common with the style of teaching which uses the koan in Zen. He drew upon most of the main religions of the world as an inspiration for his teaching, but was against what he saw as the social control exercised by many religions. He encouraged people to respond to each moment as they felt appropriate, and not to be unduly influenced by established religious doctrine.

Rajneesh opposed the socialization of the individual found in contemporary society, and wanted to free individuals to explore their own consciousness. He developed strategies for meditation, which were very different from traditional Hindu approaches, and which encouraged people to break with their personal inhibitions. He was opposed to such institutions as the family, and famously encouraged a liberal approach to sexual relations. The Rajneesh 'philosophy' did not really exist in the sense that it could be expressed as a set of rigid beliefs, or as a list of statements on personal conduct. It was an approach to supposedly living life more intensely, and to developing a greater self-awareness. It tended towards the ideal of being continually flexible and changing. His teachings have been compiled into numerous books, many of which have become influential best-sellers.

Social organization

Relatively early in the development of this new religious movement, Rajneesh began to formally induct disciples into the organization as sannyasins. In traditional Hindu society, a sannyasin is an individual who has given up all concern for the material things of life, and decided to devote himself or herself to a spiritual existence.

However, Rajneesh viewed the sannyasins in his organization, not exclusively as people who would renounce the material world, but who would also enjoy life and participate in it, besides being concerned with spiritual matters. The sannyasins wore orange robes and a set of meditation beads around their neck. At the Pune ashram the organization of a typical day tended to proceed in much the same way as typical ashram or monastery life in other Hindu or Indian traditions. There would be early morning meditation sessions, followed by other therapy or meditation classes during the day. In addition, Rajneesh would typically give a religious talk or sermon to ashram members. As the organization grew, there was a need for a more and more complex hierarchy to manage it. People in close contact with Rajneesh, who held senior positions in the movement, were able to exercise considerable power, particularly as the organization acquired considerable financial assets. Rajneesh's personal secretary, for example, seems to have had a great deal of decision-making power.

The organization established by Rajneesh has, in a somewhat different guise, continued since his death in 1990. The ashram which he founded in Pune has evolved into the Osho International Meditation Resort; a centre which runs courses on different aspects of spirituality. The Osho International Foundation is responsible for the resort and other aspects of the Osho organization.

Ethical issues

A number of ethical issues are raised by the teachings of Rajneesh and also by his life style. He was criticized by some for his liberal approach to sexual relations between people, and for his criticism of the institution of marriage. However, such a criticism depends upon those who are critical, assuming a certain moral stance which supports the received wisdom on social structure and the family. While they may argue that Rajneesh was undermining the moral fabric of society, others may argue that he was challenging accepted norms, and that this was a positive measure. The latter would no doubt take the view, that it is periodically desirable that norms are challenged, in order that society can remain in a dynamic equilibrium having the potential for change.

Some have challenged Rajneesh on his accumulation of wealth and notably the many Rolls Royces which he acquired. This seems to many to be at odds with the traditional image of the Hindu holy man, as exemplified, for example, in the image of Mahatma Gandhi. In addition, others have pointed to the very basic life style of many of the neo-sannyasins who lived on Rajneesh ashrams. In relation to this argument some have pointed to the nature of the Rajneesh organization itself, as being a large corporate structure, which became very successful as a capitalist venture. It is thus argued that this idea of capitalist accumulation of material wealth is contrary to the nature of spiritual enquiry.

Rajneesh was very supportive of the idea of freedom and liberation of the individual, in the sense that he argued that each person should decide how they wished to live their lives. His teachings tended to be very varied, drawing upon ideas from many different religions, with the result that there tended not to be a very clear coherent philosophy. The problem with this approach is that although freedom is a very attractive concept, it may be seen as not providing a sufficient moral framework within which one can live one's life.

FURTHER READING

Aitken, B. (2009) *Sri Satya Sai Baba: A Life*, London: Penguin.

Baird, R. D. (ed.) (1989) *Religion in Modern India*, New York: South Asia Publications.

Clarke, P. B. (2006) *New Religions in Global Perspective: A Study of Religious Change in the Modern World*, London: Routledge.

Mascaro, J. (1962) *The Bhagavad Gita*, London: Penguin.

Mullan, R. (1983) *Life as Laughter*, London: Routledge and Kegan Paul.

CHAPTER 4

MOVEMENTS RELATED TO CHRISTIANITY

There are many movements which have to different degrees employed Christian themes. Some have adopted a biblically fundamental approach, while others have to some extent combined Christian ideas with those from other traditions. This chapter explores four very different movements which have in various ways been inspired by the Christian message. Two of them ended in violent events, while one involves significant devotion to the ideas of a particular book. All of them, however, have drawn upon the message of Jesus Christ.

BRANCH DAVIDIAN MOVEMENT

Establishment

This new religious movement is very much connected in the public consciousness with the siege of their headquarters in Waco, Texas in 1993. On 19 April of that year, the siege of the premises by the FBI came to a violent conclusion with the death of 76 people. However, the events at Waco had a complex history, as indeed does the movement known as the Branch Davidians.

In 1935 a group which had broken away from the Seventh-day Adventist Church established themselves at Waco in Texas. They called themselves the Davidian Seventh-day Adventists, after King David in the Old Testament. In 1955 the movement divided as a result of a leadership dispute, and the Branch Davidian Seventh-day Adventists group was created under the leadership of a Benjamin Roden. The latter died in 1978, and was succeeded by his wife Lois Roden. In 1981 a 22-year-old former Seventh-day Adventist Church member, named Vernon Howell, first joined the Branch Davidian movement at Waco. In 1986 Lois Roden died and there was then a dispute between her son, George Roden, and Vernon Howell for control of the movement. Howell and some of his supporters left Waco and set up a community in a different part of Texas. Some two years later they returned to Waco, and after a complex dispute with Roden, Howell was able to gain control of the Waco community. In 1990, Howell changed his name to David Koresh. During the early 1990s suspicion and some evidence started to accumulate of the existence of a collection of weapons at the Waco centre, along with accusations of sexual exploitation. The authorities attempted to trace the weapons which had been purchased by the Branch Davidians, and became concerned that some of the guns and components purchased could have been converted into rapid-firing weapons, which would have been illegal in the hands of private citizens. In addition, local people reported that they had heard such gunfire coming from the Waco site. As a result of these concerns the local police were in contact with the Bureau of Alcohol, Tobacco and Firearms which was the official body responsible for infringements of gun use. The latter obtained a search warrant for the Branch Davidian headquarters to seek to verify if there had been any infringements of weapons legislation.

The officers of the Bureau planned to make a surprise search of the Branch Davidian buildings on 28 February 1993. However, news of the plan was leaked, and the Branch Davidians were able to arm themselves and prepare for a defensive action against the coming search. Approximately 80 members of the staff of the Bureau were involved in the projected search, but as they approached the Branch Davidian compound, gunfire erupted, and there ensued a protracted and violent gun battle which lasted for several hours. When it finally ended four officers had been killed, along with six Branch Davidians. As a result of the escalation of the conflict, and the national and international publicity, the FBI assumed control of the situation, and a large-scale siege of the Waco premises followed.

Shortly after the beginning of the siege some children were released. Protracted negotiations then started between the FBI and the Branch Davidians. However, it became clear that it would be difficult for the two sides to find common ground. As Agne (2007, p. 550) writes, 'the person-to-person interaction reveals differences in institutional identities and beliefs about God and the law, as well as attempts to work out those differences'. As the siege continued, attempts were made to cause the Davidians to surrender by cutting off water and electricity supplies. However, the fundamental problem was that Koresh called upon God as his authority, while the FBI was primarily concerned with the legal situation. Agne and Tracy (2001, p. 290) posed the following question, 'How can the negotiators show respect for the crisis partners' religious beliefs and at the same time reinforce that the government is the legitimate authority'? Eventually, after a siege lasting 50 days, the decision was taken to attack the Davidian site on 19 April. Large amounts of tear gas were used initially to try to cause the Davidians to leave the buildings. However, some appeared to have gas masks, and others were able to hide in a sealed part of the building away from the worst effects of the gas. At one stage fires started in the buildings, and spread rapidly. Some Davidians managed to escape from the fires and left the buildings, although the majority remained. The 75 adults and children who were still in the building complex died either as a result of being shot or as a consequence of the fire. David Koresh was among those who died. After the fire, some members of the movement were convicted of various charges relating to the siege. The buildings were destroyed although some Branch Davidians continued to attempt to maintain the church's activities.

Teachings

The Branch Davidians believe in the 'second coming' of Jesus Christ. They believe that Jesus will return to earth and identify a select group of righteous people who he will take back to heaven to live with him for a thousand years. After that period he will again return to earth and take with him those who are less righteous. It is believed by Branch Davidian members that there is a part of heaven where Jesus concentrates on the welfare of human beings and devotes his time to caring for the resurrection of righteous people.

The Branch Davidians hold the body in great respect as the creation of God, and as a place where the Holy Spirit can be found. They believe therefore that it is wrong to abuse the body by taking drinks which contain caffeine, alcohol or other drugs. They are also against the use of tobacco, and consider that it is wrong to eat meat.

NEW RELIGIOUS MOVEMENTS: A GUIDE FOR THE PERPLEXED

They keep Saturday as the Sabbath day, a day on which people should rest from the work of the other six days of the week. The Sabbath is in memory of the creation of the world and of all living things, by God. Branch Davidians also believe in the importance of being able to prophesy about the future. They hold that their leader should always be a person who clearly has this ability. Nevertheless, it appears that David Koresh did not adhere to all of these teachings, and adapted them when he felt necessary in order to further his control of the Branch Davidian movement.

Social organization

There is little doubt that David Koresh had a remarkable degree of control over the Branch Davidian movement. Relatively early in his relationship with the group he realized the significance of the notion of prophecy and stated that he had that gift. He also was apparently an impressive and persuasive speaker, who was able to use an extensive knowledge of the Bible in order to support his claims and arguments. So dominant and manipulative a personality was he, that his congregation soon became very dependent on him and his organizing powers. He created the impression that the movement was to some extent under siege from the outside world, and that everyone else was against them. This provided him with the rationale to arm the group so heavily, as he persuaded all the members that they would have to defend themselves at some point, against attacks from outside. Ironically perhaps, it was the sound of members practising with their guns, which caused neighbours of the Waco property to be suspicious about the intentions of the group.

Koresh appears to have had a greatly inflated sense of his own importance, and particularly in a religious and spiritual sense. He appears to have believed that he was ordained to be the religious leader of the Branch Davidians and in a distorted interpretation of the Old Testament believed this gave him the right to have multiple sexual partners within the group members. It does appear that members of the group had a deep and genuine belief in their faith, and that they were prepared to defend their faith in a confrontation, if attacked. It is difficult to assess whether this was due simply to religious conviction or to a degree of manipulation by David Koresh.

Ethical issues

A wide range of ethical issues are raised by the degree of control which David Koresh appears to have had over the Branch Davidian group. On the one hand, those members who stayed in the Waco property towards the end of the siege appear to have done so of their own volition. They seem to have been very committed to the Davidian faith and some even to have been prepared to die in its defence. It is arguable, however, whether this was an autonomous decision on the part of some, or whether they were in effect indoctrinated by David Koresh. Even if a degree of autonomy were evident in the decision-making of the adults, there were a considerable number of children and adolescents in the Waco centre who arguably were not of a degree of maturity to exercise such maturity. It would appear unethical to place them in a situation where their lives were endangered for a religious cause which they were not in a position to fully comprehend. It does seem that the Branch Davidians under the leadership of David Koresh possessed many of the characteristics of a closed community, which lacked the balancing effects of contact with the outside world. They accepted extremes of behaviour, partly because they did not possess external points of reference to help them evaluate what was happening in their community. This was particularly so with respect to the sexual relations which David Koresh seems to have had with women in the community, some of whom were married to male members of the Davidians. In addition, he seems also to have had relations with, and fathered children by, young adolescent girls, in the community. It is very difficult to see how this could have happened unless Koresh had such a remarkable degree of control over the members that they acquiesced to behaviour patterns which most people would regard as ethically abnormal.

STUDY QUESTION

This community under David Koresh's leadership provides an exemplar of the dangers of a group of people leading an enclosed, isolated existence in the presence of a manipulative and dominating personality. Can you think of any other examples of 'closed' communities or societies in which people tend to behave in an irrational or non-conventional way?

The history of the Waco siege also provides an example of the difficulty demonstrated by agencies of society, in communicating effectively with such communities. As Eisenhart (2006, p. 165) argues, 'the government experts and decision makers fail to marshal any theological expertise to understand the religious perspective of the Davidians at Waco.'

A COURSE IN MIRACLES

Establishment

'A Course in Miracles' is the title of a book rather than the name of a new religious movement, although it is a convenient term to describe those people who devote themselves both to the study of the book and to the application of its principles. The book was first published in 1975 and since then has sold somewhere between one and a half million and two million copies. It has created an international body of devotees and followers.

The principal person in the origin of the book was Dr Helen Schucman who was born in 1909 and died in 1981. In 1965 she was a clinical psychologist and associate professor at Columbia University in New York. A remark by her colleague, Professor William Thetford appears to have stimulated a chain of events which resulted in the writing of *A Course in Miracles*. Helen Schucman began to feel the presence of a voice within her that motivated her to write down a series of religious observations about the world, which in effect constituted advice on ways in which human beings could lead more fulfilled and rewarding lives. She felt that the voice came from Jesus. William Thetford supported her in this process. The writing of the book was completed after approximately seven years, in 1972. There remains a debate to be had about whether the internal voice experienced by Helen Schucman was actually that of the historical Jesus, in effect dictating a message to her, or whether it was a spiritual reflection of the message of Jesus within her.

Helen Schucman was a serious academic, as was William Thetford. She does not appear to have been a practising religious person, although at the same time she seems to have had a continuing interest in spirituality and mysticism. The writing process was completed and the book first published in 1975 by an organization called The Foundation for Inner Peace. Interestingly the book is not registered as having an author. Helen Schucman did not wish to be considered the author since she felt the words had come from Jesus. Equally it was not possible to identify Jesus as the author. Since the initial publication of *A Course in Miracles* there have also been copyright disputes about the book, due in part to the lack of clarity over authorship.

Teachings

A Course in Miracles (ACIM) consists of three main texts. The principal text is the actual course document. This is accompanied by a Workbook for Students which provides a series of progressive lessons, and by A Manual for Teachers, which provides advice for those who would act in the role of counsellor or adviser to students. The actual course document provides a large number of spiritual statements designed to help the reader to rethink their lives. The Workbook for Students translates these sometimes theoretical and perhaps rather obscure statements of principle into practical strategies and actions for the reader. The entire approach of ACIM is to encourage people to view the world and to interact with it, in a different and more positive way.

The analysis of the programme is that there are two different types of knowledge in the world. One of these is the absolute knowledge generated by God and God's actions in the world. If we turn to God then we begin to see the real nature of the world, with a sense of love and devotion. We perceive the world and our fellow human beings as they truly are. On the other hand, there is a different type of knowledge which is relative rather than absolute. It is created by human beings through their interaction with the world, and is profoundly affected by the way in which they perceive the world around them. In particular it is affected by their upbringing and their social conditioning. We all tend to make sense of the world as a result partly of our socialization and partly of our genetic make-up. However, what ACIM is arguing is that this type of relative interpretation of the world will not only vary from one human being to another, but will lack the profound and absolute understanding of the world which is based upon the love of God. The latter is seen as being capable of transforming our approach to life, and providing us with a new vision of the world.

The argument of the Course is that the relativistic world which we create for ourselves is based partly on our own attitudes and volition. We want the world and other people to be as we want them to be. We try to impose our own hopes and aspirations on the world, and struggle to make it as we wish it. Ultimately however, this is a vain aspiration, and the world view resulting from such an approach is an aberration of the real, absolute world of God.

However, according to ACIM, we are not really to be blamed for this rather selfish approach to life. Nor should we blame ourselves. However, what we should do is to try to change our approach to life so that we act in tune with the Holy Spirit, and behave with genuine love towards the world. Such love is a profound affection and respect for others, which wants to give of ourselves, rather than gain things for ourselves.

One of the difficulties of a relativistic, egocentric approach to existence is that it can generate a sense of fear about the world. We are anxious that things will go wrong, that the world will fail to be what we would like, and that people will let us down. However, once we transform this view, to one based upon the love of God, then this anxiety and stress disappears to a large extent, being replaced by a peaceful and more positive world view.

The title of the work, *A Course in Miracles*, comes from the idea of this complete change in the perception of the world, which is regarded as indeed miraculous. The relativistic view tends to separate us from other people, and to place us in conflict with others. We can sometimes imagine that others are being unpleasant to us, when in fact it is merely that they are suffering in some way, and not behaving as they would really like to do. If we are in tune with the Holy Spirit, then we do not over-react in such circumstances, and we behave in a much more positive way.

A Course in Miracles tends to employ Christian concepts to explain its teachings. However, in some ways there is a divergence between Christianity and this approach. Perhaps notable is the emphasis in ACIM upon the individual being responsible for the changes necessary in revising our view of the world. We have to be dependent on ourselves and be determined to alter our perception of the world. In a sense we are less dependent upon the intervention of Jesus Christ, and more dependent upon transforming ourselves. The difference is perhaps more a matter of emphasis, but it nevertheless is seen by some as a demarcation between orthodox Christianity and ACIM.

Social organization

A Course in Miracles does not have the same type of social organization as many other new religious movements, but nevertheless has a network of people who are committed to its study. There are, for example, a great many study groups which have formed in different countries, where like-minded people meet to discuss the principles involved in the course. The Foundation for Inner Peace has continued its publishing activities, and has published a further collection of materials relevant to the course. A separate organization, The Foundation for a Course in Miracles, was established in 1983 principally to develop mechanisms for teaching and delivering ACIM. The Foundation later established in 1995, the Institute for Teaching Inner Peace through a Course in Miracles.

The Course has now been translated into a number of different languages, and is clearly attracting interest on a worldwide scale. Other organizations which are committed to teaching the principles of ACIM have evolved, and offer a range of teaching materials, including computer-based programmes.

Ethical issues

Arguably the central moral issue of ACIM is the definition of 'sin' which is offered. If we commit a selfish or egocentric act designed to further our own gain or pleasure at the expense of others, this would traditionally, within a Christian perspective, be viewed as a sin. However, within the perspective of the Course, it is seen rather more as a failure to perceive the true nature of the world in terms of God's love and of the Holy Spirit. It is the result of a failure to comprehend the nature of truth and love. Rather than suggest that someone is 'guilty' of a sin, people are encouraged to try to change their understanding of the world so that they can act in a more loving and considerate way to their fellow human beings. People should be encouraged to forgive others and to forgive themselves, but not to carry an oppressive burden of guilt for alleged wrongdoings.

This can be perceived as a very kind and gentle approach to morality. One is taught to view the world in a way which encourages a less egocentric and selfish way of acting towards others – one which is based upon an unconditional love for the human condition.

THE PEOPLES TEMPLE

Establishment

The Peoples Temple was founded by James Jones in 1956, although there had been previous organizations which led to the development of the Peoples Temple. Jim Jones was born in Indiana in 1931, and he appears to have grown up with a strong interest in, and commitment to, social equality issues. In parallel with this commitment, he also became interested in communism, particularly in relation to its message of equality for all people and all ethnic groups. In 1954 Jim Jones started to preach at a Methodist Church in Indiana, and tried to increase the number of Afro-Americans who attended the church. This antagonized many of the long-established church members and Jones decided to leave the church. In 1956 he set up his own church according to his principles of equality and of placing a high priority on helping the poor and socially disadvantaged. This church was named the Wings of Deliverance, and later in 1956 became the Peoples Temple. The church combined an implicit socialism and politically left-wing, social activism, with a Christian theology. However, the politics of Indiana at the time was profoundly against ethnic integration, and partly in order to find a more tolerant environment in which to develop the Temple, Jones decided to move the Church headquarters to California. This was accomplished by 1965, and by 1972 a church had also been established in San Francisco. A great many social projects were established at this time, providing food donations and medical assistance for poorer sections of society. In addition, more Afro-Caribbean members joined the Church.

During the early 1970s there commenced, however, some criticisms of the Peoples Temple. There were suggestions that its financial arrangements were somewhat irregular, and also some people left the Church, only later to argue that it contained many of the elements of a cult. These pressures on the Church may have been a key factor in persuading Jones that a move outside the United States might be an appropriate development for the Temple. The country of Guyana in South America was identified as a potential location for the future evolution of the Church. Guyana had at the time a government which was politically left-wing and supportive of the social principles of the Peoples Temple. English was also the lingua franca, which helped communication and the administrative aspects of the Temple. By

1974 the decision had finally been taken to move to Guyana, and the Temple obtained a large area of land for its use, on which to establish a religious community. Jones and other members who moved there saw this as a possibility to create a community which would grow its own food and be largely self-sustaining. It would also be able to flourish in a supportive environment away from the developing criticism in the United States. In 1977, James Jones and some other Temple members moved to Guyana to live in the community which was now informally known as Jonestown. The community grew to about 1,000 members. Life at Jonestown was almost certainly very hard physically, with a great deal of agricultural work to be done, along with fund-raising, and the necessity to provide child-care and educational arrangements. Some people left Jonestown, and when back in the United States began to systematically criticize the Peoples Temple. There were suggestions, for example, that some members wanted to leave Jonestown but were in various ways prevented from doing so. A member of the United States Congress, Leo J. Ryan, was persuaded to take an interest in Jonestown and the way in which the Peoples Temple was organized. Ryan and a small team of colleagues set off for Guyana in mid-November 1978. On 17 November Ryan was able to tour the Jonestown complex and to interview some residents. During the tour it became clear that some members wanted to leave and they asked Leo Ryan to provide them with assistance. On the following day, 18 November, Ryan managed to organize a small group of people who wished to fly with him to the United States. They travelled to a small local airport in order to fly to the capital of Guyana on the first stage of their journey home. However, they were followed by armed members of the Peoples Temple who fired at Leo Ryan and his group. Ryan and four others were killed, and a number of people seriously injured.

The shooting precipitated a crisis at Jonestown, and James Jones clearly realized that intervention by the Guyanese and American authorities would be very rapid. He had long suggested the notion of a mass suicide as a possibility if the group was threatened, and now put this into action. A large amount of a mixture of fruit drink and cyanide was prepared, and members told to administer it to children, and then take it themselves. It seems probable that many parents poisoned their own children. Analysis of Jonestown after the event suggests that some people may have been shot. In total, just over 900 people died at Jonestown.

In hindsight it seems a completely irrational act to commit mass suicide. The context however was one of an isolated community who believed they were constructing a more positive lifestyle away from the influence of a capitalist, oppressive state. When the existence of this was threatened, they were conditioned to believe that everything for which they had worked would inevitably be destroyed, and that death was the only realistic end; as Dein and Littlewood (2005, p. 205) put it 'violence is precipitated through the actual or perceived interaction of the apocalyptic group with the host community'. They decided largely that death was preferable to seeing the collapse of their community, along with the investigation into the deaths of Leo Ryan and his colleagues. Such a view makes little sense in the context of the rational outside world, but within the closed community of Jonestown, given the indoctrination to which people were subjected, one can imagine how people could react in this way.

Teachings

From the beginning James Jones was influenced by the Pentecostal Church. He supported the idea of the 'Second Coming' of Jesus Christ, and advocated faith healing and the skills of prophecy. It appears likely that with the assistance of some members, acts of faith healing were exaggerated. Such instances were used to impress potential members, and to further recruitment to the Temple. It appears though that some supporters of the Temple had a genuine belief in the power of Jones to heal people through faith. It equally appears probable that examples of 'prophecy' were created by conspiring to 'reveal' information about people which could have been obtained by other means. This again was employed as a means of influencing and impressing people, and hence for enhancing donations to the Temple or for obtaining new members.

There appears to have been, therefore, a degree of exploitation of religion in order to both increase the number of members and also in parallel augment the financial income to the organization. The latter was used to support the extensive range of social support mechanisms for the elderly, the disadvantaged and the sick. The ideological basis for this was a combination of communism and socialism. This was initially combined with and related to some of Jesus Christ's ethical teachings about helping others. However, as time progressed, Jones began to undermine the orthodox Christian elements of his teaching, and to enhance the social ethics elements of what he taught. He continued, for example, to support the increased membership of Afro-Caribbean people. As his personal influence expanded within the Temple community, and as the Christian influence diminished, Jones began to propose himself as a sort of divine figure, and even suggested that he himself was in fact, the 'Second Coming'. He began to assume the role of a classical cult leader, with extreme and wide-ranging influence over his members. This ultimately led to the irrational leadership and manipulative style evident at Jonestown.

Social organization

One of the basic features of the Peoples Temple organization created by Jones was that he encouraged a form of social cooperative, whereby every member was asked to contribute all of their financial assets to the community. These assets were then combined and distributed to those in need. The elderly, sick or disadvantaged were assessed in terms of their needs, and received money or medical treatment as necessary. The combined assets of the Temple were also used to finance the many social help programmes which were initiated in the broader community.

The Peoples Temple had a complex committee structure, with each committee providing a forum within which certain types of decision could be taken. Although there was a considerable degree of participation within this committee structure, there was nevertheless, a hierarchical decision-making process. The Temple members included a number of professionally qualified or university-educated people whose skills were utilized by Jones in order to manage, for example, the financial and legal aspects of the Temple organization. Such well-educated members would also have been very useful in furthering the image of the Temple among the many external organizations with which the Temple had contact. The Temple cultivated links with politicians and the press, and in some of these relationships at least, it created a positive impression. During the period in California, the Temple also had a positive working relationship with different aspects of the social services provision administered by the state. This assisted the Temple in establishing its own social care network. It is interesting that the Peoples Temple employed an apparently religious message and teaching in order to develop a social programme with an underlying political, and in this case socialist, doctrine. This appears to be relatively unusual in the context of new religious movements.

Ethical issues

On a certain level, one of the most striking aspects of the Peoples Temple, particularly in its early stages of development, was its emphasis upon social moral issues. James Jones strongly supported racial equality and integration, at a time when there was considerable opposition to this principle. Not only did he support the principle of racial equality, but he tried to put this principle into practice by recruiting black members of his church congregation even though this created much opposition. He also remained, for most of the history of the Temple, an advocate and practical supporter of the needs of the disadvantaged, the poor and the handicapped. It could be argued that in this policy Jones was following a political ideology rather than an ethical imperative for its own sake, but at least the result was that many people in need were helped. However, this range of social provision required a good deal of financial support, and the mechanisms used to generate this, could certainly be questioned on moral grounds. The Temple mounted 'healing' demonstrations of improbable validity in order to gain support, and also sold religious artefacts of doubtful use.

Finally, as the Temple developed, and particularly after the move to Guyana, it tended to become more and more autocratic as an organization. It demanded a strong sense of loyalty on the part of members and refused to accept any dissent. A range of sanctions and punishments evolved to try to encourage people to accept the official doctrines of the Temple. The ethics of this was certainly questionable, on the grounds that the autonomy and freedom of individuals were reduced. One could also argue that indoctrination was an important element in persuading members to accept official Temple policies.

THE UNIFICATION CHURCH

Establishment

The Unification Church was founded in South Korea by Sun Myung Moon in 1954. Followers of the Church have often been referred to colloquially in recent years as 'Moonies' after the name of the founder, although this term has developed a rather negative connotation. Members of the Church tend to prefer that it is not used. When the Church was first established, its full name was 'The Holy Spirit Association for the Unification of World Christianity'.

Sun Myung Moon was born in 1920 in North Korea. Initially the family followed Confucian teachings, but later became Christians and members of the Presbyterian Church. In 1935 Moon had a vision in which Jesus Christ asked him to continue his teaching on earth. During the period of the Second World War he studied in Japan, but returned to Korea when the war was over. He occasionally made statements about politics and religion which made him unpopular with the Korean government. As a result of this he served periods in prison and in labour camps, which he was fortunate enough to survive. After establishing in 1954 the Unification Church which spread rapidly, Moon was soon in a position to send members abroad to spread his teachings. A new member of the Church at this time was a young lady named Young Oon Kim. She became a missionary of the Church in the United States, and established herself in the State of Oregon. Eventually the Church moved to California, where further converts were gained. Meanwhile the movement was also expanding considerably in Japan. In 1960 Moon was married to Hak Ja Han. It was the third time he had been married. Hak Ja Han is often termed the 'True Mother' by Church members, and their children as the 'True Children'.

Expansion continued throughout the 1960s and into the 1970s. The Church attracted a diverse membership of young people, including some from the 1960s hippie movement. A great emphasis was placed upon the willingness of new members to participate in money-raising ventures. By the beginning of the 1970s, the Reverend Moon (as he is frequently known in the press and in the Church itself) became more and more involved in politics. He gave support to the United States president, Richard Nixon, during the so-called Watergate scandal, and in general supported politically right-wing causes. The Unification Movement was by now very wealthy from donations and other fund-raising activities, and was able to exert considerable influence. In 1982 the Reverend Moon was accused and convicted of income tax irregularities in the United States, but some commentators considered that the financial arrangements of the Unification movement were in essence no different from those of a number of other religious organizations. The Reverend Moon was hence viewed, at the very least within his own organization, as having been the subject of an unfair prosecution. In subsequent years as he got older, the Reverend Moon has gradually encouraged his children to assume more and more responsibility for the Unification movement.

Teachings

The key religious teachings of the movement are contained in the text 'The Divine Principle'. The Unification Church believes in the existence of one true God who is the creator of the universe and also of men and women. God embraces the principles and characteristics of both the male and female genders. God also represents all of the good and desirable ethical principles of the universe. It is accepted that Jesus Christ, as the son of God, came down to earth to atone for the sins of human beings and to start to create the divine kingdom on earth.

According to the Unification movement, the goal of spiritual life is for human beings to lead a life which is united with God. In the context of the Unification Church, Collins (2000, p. 329) argues that 'we all share a common ancestry dating back to the first two human beings and must learn how to treat everyone as if he or she is a member of our extended family'. Unfortunately, such a life is very difficult for men and women because they have been influenced by immoral and unethical tendencies. They require the intervention of Jesus to forgive their sins and to help them move closer to God in the way in which they lead their lives. All human beings have the capacity to reunite themselves with God. Although God gives this potential to human beings, the latter must exercise their own self-determination in deciding that they would like to live in closer unity with God. If they decide to work hard to achieve this, then, with the help of Jesus Christ and of the Holy Spirit, they can experience a form of spiritual reawakening. The Bible is perceived as a historical account of the way in which God has encouraged, with the help of his Son, people to re-evaluate their lives and develop a stronger sense of spirituality. Members of the Unification movement believe in the Second Coming of Jesus Christ, during the present historical period. This Second Coming will initiate a new era for human beings, one of a closer union of God and humanity.

Social organization

The structure and organization of the Unification movement clearly centres around the Reverend Moon. This may be viewed both as a strength and as a weakness of the organization. On the one hand, it provides a sense of strong, central, theological leadership; while on the other, it may be viewed as resulting in a rather controlling, autocratic approach. Moon has claimed, for example, that he represents the Second Coming of Christ, and that he is really present on earth to bring salvation to the entire population of the world. In common with many leaders of new religious movements, the Reverend Moon has an extremely affluent lifestyle. The financial basis of the organization is apparently complex, and the movement is linked with a number of major commercial enterprises. The Unification Church owns a major newspaper, *The Washington Times*, which is arguably influential among relatively right-wing United States politicians. This presence in the news media provides the movement with contacts and a degree of influence in political circles. The movement also owns several significant business corporations in Japan and Korea. Individual members of the movement are asked to give generously of their own assets to the movement.

The large-scale marriage or blessing ceremony is a well-known feature of the Unification Church. Many thousands of couples will typically participate in such ceremonies. Some may already be married and will be using the ceremony to in effect affirm their commitment to each other. Others may be 'engaged', and following the mass ceremony will later be formally and legally married during a secular ceremony. Some couples are actually put in touch with each other through the Unification Church, and sometimes the Reverend Moon may affirm the selection. The Reverend Moon and the Church as a whole are very antagonistic to homosexuality, and will not condone couples of the same sex taking part in these large-scale blessing ceremonies.

Ethical issues

A central ethical issue for the organization is that its essential religious nature may be confused with its major commercial enterprises. It may be difficult for some people to accept these two functions as existing in harmony. A church whose religious message often involves the ethics of helping the poor and disadvantaged may seem incongruous, when viewed from the perspective of a major financial conglomeration. For example, the Church has bought large areas of land in South America, for a variety of commercial and development purposes. This has arguably had a deleterious effect upon the lives of the indigenous inhabitants. Overall, it is somewhat difficult to view this type of policy as essentially ethical.

The Unification Church is an enormous worldwide organization, and as with all such organizations, there will inevitably be some varieties of practice. However, the Church has come under criticism at times for its methods of recruiting and retaining new members, which have been seen as overly controlling and perhaps manipulative. There have also been some claims of excessive persuasion of people to contribute financially to the Church. The Reverend Moon has, however, been a consistent and strong advocate of world peace, and has also increasingly tried to relate to other key world faiths.

FURTHER READING

Bryant, M. D. and Richardson, H. W. (eds) (1978) *A Time for Consideration: A Scholarly Appraisal of the Unification Church*, New York: Edwin Mellen Press.

Hong, N. (1998) *In the Shadow of the Moons: My Life in the Reverend Sun Myung Moon's Family*, Boston: Little, Brown.

Newport, K. G. C. (2006) *The Branch Davidians of Waco: The History and Beliefs of an Apocalyptic Sect*, Oxford: Oxford University Press.

Reavis, D. J. (1995) *The Ashes of Waco: An Investigation*, New York: Simon and Schuster.

Wright, S. A. (ed.) (1995) *Armageddon in Waco: Critical Perspectives on the Branch Davidian Conflict*, Chicago: University of Chicago Press.

CHAPTER 5

MOVEMENTS RELATED TO BUDDHISM

This chapter discusses three new religious movements, two of which are Buddhist, and one, Falun Gong, which incorporates elements of Buddhism. Both Theravada and Mahayana Buddhist traditions continue to be popular in the West, with many opportunities in monasteries and Buddhist centres to learn meditational techniques and Buddhist teachings.

THE TRIRATNA BUDDHIST COMMUNITY

Establishment

The Triratna Buddhist Community is a new religious movement which was previously known as the Friends of the Western Buddhist Order. It was established in 1967 as a movement devoted to developing Buddhism in a contemporary Western context. The founder of the movement was Dennis Lingwood, whose Buddhist name is Sangharakshita. As a young man he was stationed in India during the Second World War, and was able to further his interest in Buddhism. After the war he was ordained as a Buddhist monk, and was also a student at Benares Hindu University. From the early 1950s onwards Sangharakshita lived in northern India at Kalimpong where he established a Buddhist organization, and furthered his contacts with Tibetan Buddhists, and those from other Buddhist traditions. It was at about this time that he met Dr Ambedkar, the leader of the then-termed 'untouchables' in India. Many from this disadvantaged group had undergone, or were in the process of, conversion to Buddhism, and Sangharakshita did a great deal to encourage this process. He returned to England initially in 1964, and later in 1967 founded the Friends of the Western Buddhist Order. Sangharakshita wanted to retain the essential teachings of historical Buddhism, and also acknowledge that Buddhism had always to some extent assumed the cultural characteristics of the context in which it developed. He wanted to develop a form of Buddhist practice which would seem relevant to people in Western countries. In addition, he sought to draw upon the different major schools of Buddhism, in order to create a tradition which had wide relevance. The movement gradually expanded into a worldwide organization with many members, particularly in India. Sangharakshita retired in 1995, and in 1997 the management of the organization was assumed by a form of executive committee.

Teachings

The Triratna Buddhist Community is distinguished firstly by an eclectic approach in terms of being prepared to recognize the diversity of practice within the Buddhist world, but also by developing a new variety of practice which does not rely upon existing tradition. Sangharakshita tried to delineate the aspects of Buddhism which were at the core of the religion, such as the practice of taking refuge in the 'Three Jewels' of the Buddha, Dharma and the Sangha. The dharma is the concept which embraces the teachings of the Buddha, with a particular significance devoted to the Four Noble Truths.

The movement places a great emphasis upon meditation, commencing with the development of mindfulness through learning to concentrate upon the in and out motion of the breath. This has the effect of calming the mind and making it receptive to the development of insight through meditation. Through this process the person is able to gradually develop an appreciation of the impermanence of the world, and that a distorted understanding of this can lead to suffering. In addition, through insight the individual begins to appreciate that he or she does not have a permanent identity, and that failure to understand the non-existence of the self can also result in suffering. The movement also teaches the importance of developing a spirit of loving kindness towards others. This is created partly through the meditation process, and focusing upon the way in which showing kindness to others can help reduce suffering. One should also demonstrate kindness to oneself, in the sense of not being overly critical on the occasions when we fail to match up to our goals or aspirations. The movement also emphasizes the benefits of cultivating a community of Buddhists who provide friendship and support for each other.

STUDY QUESTION

In traditional schools of Buddhism there is normally a distinction between monks and nuns who are ordained and lay people who have not sought ordination. In the Triratna community, however, there is a single ordination process which to some extent combines the characteristics of the ordained and lay existence. In orthodox Buddhism, the Vinaya or monastic code of conduct provided strict rules governing the conduct of monks and nuns. Try to find out about the Vinaya. Apart from providing a moral code, how might the Vinaya affect the relationship between ordained and lay Buddhists?

Social organization

Sangharakshita has been at the heart of the movement's organization since its inception in 1967. He has encouraged members of the movement to be 'engaged' in society by supporting ventures which help the disadvantaged. He has interpreted Buddhism for those who may have found traditional models of the religion to be too complex.

The movement places a great emphasis upon the collective membership of the Triratna community. The movement argues that individuals can gain a great deal in terms of spiritual development from the interaction within a Buddhist community. The community-centred spiritual development takes place within retreats, and within more permanent living arrangements. Members of the Triratna movement work together on charitable projects, and on ethically based, fund-raising ventures. The movement also arranges many meditation classes for existing members and also to spread an understanding of Buddhism to newcomers.

Ethical issues

In the Theravada tradition it is normal for ordained monks and nuns to abstain from being involved in commercial activities. The form of ordination which has evolved in the Triratna community involves both ordained and lay norms and values, and hence members of the community may find themselves participating in activities in order to raise money for the organization. The potential ethical issue here is that constant vigilance is required in order to maintain the moral dimension to 'ethical trading' for example, in order to place the emphasis upon the purpose of the fund-raising, rather than simply trying to accumulate as much money as possible. The Triratna philosophy in terms of collective working is to as far as possible ensure that all aspects of the business are ethical, and that the Buddhist workers are paid sufficiently to sustain a reasonable level of existence. This then should leave sufficient funds to support the various social and educational projects developed by the community. The notion of an engaged Buddhist is thus a person who not only commits to the Buddha's teachings, but also tries, through putting those principles into practice, to improve the nature of fairness and equality in society. As Baumann (1998, p. 132) argues, 'the aim of a Right Livelihood business is thus, apart from its economic efficiency and producing a financial surplus, to change the existing society.'

The Triratna Buddhist Community has thus tried to adhere to traditional Buddhist values while at the same time trying to situate these values within a rapidly changing Western society.

FALUN GONG

Establishment

Falun Gong is an eclectic spiritual, religious and moral system which was developed in China in 1992. It is also known as Falun Dafa. It synthesizes aspects of Buddhism and Daoism, and the practical philosophy of qigong. Hence, although it may legitimately be considered as a new religious movement, it is based upon traditional Chinese spiritual principles. Spiritual systems associated with qigong became very popular in China in the late 1980s and 1990s. Qi is the term used to describe the energy which is present in the body. Qigong is any system of practice, whether physical or spiritual, which seeks to enhance the functioning of qi in the body. Such practices may involve meditation, physical exercises of various kinds including those associated with martial arts, or special dietary practices.

The movement was founded by Li Hongzhi in 1992. Details of his early life are not easy to define with any precision, but it appears that his parents were not particularly affluent, and that he was born in either 1951 or 1952. It seems that he received tuition from Buddhist and Daoist teachers when he was young, but that as he grew older, he did not hold any especially high-status jobs. Li Hongzhi developed the integration of classical Chinese systems of thought during the late 1980s, and then presented Falun Gong in the town of Changchun in 1992. As a system of thought and practice, it was immediately, extremely popular, and Li proceeded to give many lectures all over China, discussing the philosophical ideas of Falung Gong as well as the meditational and physical exercises. He has consistently tried to divert attention from his own biography, since he argues that his own existence is of no particular significance, but the teachings of Falun Gong are much more important. In 1998 Li moved to the United States.

During the early stages of development, Falun Gong attracted a membership from all sections of society, including apparently members of the communist party. There was at this time no evidence of the antagonism between the Chinese government and Falun Gong, which would arise later. Between 1996 and 1998 Falun Gong may have attracted as many as 100 million members, and yet this did not appear to cause unease to the government. However, it was during this period that the beginnings of adverse press coverage started to take place. It is difficult to know whether this was motivated by feelings in the government. If so, then it may have been an ideological clash between communist thinking and comments made by Li, or alternatively it may have been concerns over the sheer size of the Falun Gong membership.

In April 1999 a very large number of Falun Gong members protested in Beijing. There may have been as many as 10,000 people present. They were protesting specifically against the arrest, earlier in the year, of a small group of demonstrators in the town of Tianjin. The protestors sat around government buildings in Tiananmen Square, and it may have been this challenge to the government which brought about a reaction. In any case, later that year the government outlawed Falun Gong and commenced a period of repression of the movement.

Many aspects of the rise of the Falun Gong may have disturbed the government. Given the size of the April 1999 demonstration, the government may have suspected that senior figures in the country, indeed members of the establishment, were supporters of Falun Gong. This perhaps contributed to the determination of the Chinese government to mount an oppressive campaign against Falun Gong. The government argued that Falun Gong was propagating a philosophy which was in total opposition to the values and approach of the communist party. The campaign against Falun Gong was put into operation throughout the mass media, while Li Hongzhi and his colleagues tried to counter the accusations from abroad. The government campaign tried to argue that Falun Gong had many of the same characteristics as the cults in the West. As the repression increased in intensity, it seems likely that some members were subjected to serious ill-treatment. In the intervening time peaceful protests and demonstrations have continued in China, even though the penalties for those arrested were considerable. Falun Gong has also continued with its overseas demonstrations and attempts to draw the attention of the public around the world to the plight of Falun Gong members in China.

Teachings

The three fundamental moral concepts of Falun Gong teaching are truthfulness, compassion and forbearance. These concepts are discussed in the two definitive books of Falun Gong, namely 'Falun Gong' and 'Zhuan Falun'. The latter in particular explains the concept of 'cultivation'. Li Hongzhi explains that the principal spiritual purpose of Falun Gong is the cultivation of the above moral qualities. He argues that these qualities are an intrinsic element of the universe, and that the true destiny of human beings is to bring themselves into empathy with these moral qualities. In some ways it would appear as if cultivation of truthfulness, compassion and forbearance will result in an improved orientation of qi in the body, a process not dissimilar from the Daoist trying to exist in harmony with the Dao. One of the key strategies to be adopted, according to Master Li, is the practice of non-attachment. This is also an important Buddhist concept which stems from an understanding of impermanence. Once the practitioner realizes that all things, living and non-living, are impermanent, it is easier to be less-attached to them. It tends to stop us wanting the things which other people may have, because we understand the impermanence of such things. It also tends to stop us being as competitive as we might be because the material things which we acquire are not perceived as having any ultimate permanence.

Social organization

It is very difficult to establish with certainty the organizational structure of Falun Gong because of the widely disparate accounts which are available. The Chinese government tends to perceive it as having a complex, hierarchical structure, with authority disseminated downwards through a series of management strata. It also portrays Falun Gong as having considerable financial assets acquired through fees and contributions from members. The Falun Gong organization portrays itself in a very different way, arguing that it is a highly decentralized and informal structure, with a very limited hierarchical arrangement. It argues that its local study and meditation groups are largely autonomous, perhaps using books and recordings from the organization for study purposes, but mainly depending upon its own resources. Falun Gong asserts that it does not charge fees for its tuition in local groups, and does not accumulate excessive financial resources as claimed by the Chinese government. It also claims that there are no strict criteria for membership, and no membership formalities. Hence it is difficult to establish accurate membership data.

It may be that in the early 1990s, Falun Gong did in fact develop a fairly complex organization, but that this was gradually reduced as it came under greater and greater pressure from the Chinese government. Although Falun Gong tried to be accepted as a recognized organization, it did not receive such approval. The gradual dispersal of its organization, such as it was, may have been a defence mechanism against the charges by the Chinese government that it was a formal challenge to the Chinese system. It is perhaps also worth noting that members of Falun Gong do not need to formally accept a particular belief system when they join. There are no specific beliefs or point of faith to which members must declare agreement. It is, therefore, not easy to define with certainty, who is, and who is not, a member.

There is clearly a conflictual situation existing between Falun Gong and the Chinese government, and at the same time both parties are seeking to portray the other in a certain light. One might hypothesize therefore that it is understandable that the Chinese government should portray Falun Gong as a large-scale, autocratic hierarchy; and equally that Falun Gong should seek to explain itself as an informal, decentralized and rather amorphous organization.

Ethical issues

Falun Gong has a strong ethical dimension to its teachings, and as mentioned above the most important concepts are forbearance, truthfulness and compassion. Falun Gong members are encouraged to practise meditation and non-attachment in order to enhance these moral qualities. The practice of non-attachment is similar to that of traditional Buddhism, where individuals try to distance themselves from the material things of life. By doing this Falun Gong argues that they will be more able to have compassion for others. Non-violence is also a central tenet of the movement. In the demonstrations by the organization against the actions of the Chinese government, a policy of non-violence has always been adopted. Forbearance is a very necessary quality to practise in the light of the oppression of members by the Chinese authorities.

Falun Gong has been criticized for its negative attitude towards homosexuals, although it normally appears to admit them to membership. It seems that the organization does not insist upon standard religious beliefs which have to be accepted by all members. There is thus a generally liberal approach to beliefs, which encourages individuals to explore their own views about issues, rather than adopting fixed and rigid views.

THE NEW KADAMPA TRADITION – INTERNATIONAL KADAMPA BUDDHIST UNION

Establishment

The New Kadampa Tradition was established by Geshe Kelsang Gyatso in 1991. It is a worldwide organization with a large number of centres in different countries. Geshe Kelsang left Tibet in 1959 for India. In 1976 he was invited by his own guru to become a teacher at the Manjushri Institute in the United Kingdom. During a long period of meditation which ended in 1991, Geshe Kelsang thought out the basis of the organization which would become the New Kadampa Tradition – International Kadampa Buddhist

Union. The organization was formally established in 1992, and Geshe Kelsang remained as head of the New Kadampa Tradition until his retirement in 2009.

The organization is distinctively Tibetan in its religious and cultural inheritance, and has evolved from the Gelug School. The teachings may be traced back to the eleventh-century Tibetan teacher, Atisha, and the fifteenth-century teacher, Je Tsongkhapa. The intention of Geshe Kelsang when establishing the New Kadampa was to create a Buddhist organization which would appear relevant to Westerners, and to people living in the contemporary world. In addition, he wanted to ensure that people did not simply study Tibetan Buddhism from an academic point of view, but learned how to extend this knowledge through meditation and practical Buddhist experience. In its relatively short history the organization has been very successful at disseminating its teachings, and has experienced very rapid growth. Geshe Kelsang has written over 20 books elaborating on his teachings, and these have proved very popular.

Teachings

The teachings of the New Kadampa Tradition are largely embraced within what is termed the Mahayana tradition of Buddhism. The Theravada tradition, today largely found in south-east Asia, is characterized by a concentration upon gaining an understanding of the true nature of the world, and hence of being enlightened. The Mahayana tradition, while following the same fundamental teachings as the Theravada, focuses primarily upon the responsibility of the individual to help all other beings achieve enlightenment.

All forms of Buddhism concentrate upon the importance of the mind, and upon controlling the mind. The mind is seen as the potential cause of much suffering. It is often supposed that it is the material world which is the cause of our suffering. In other words, if we do not have the possessions which we would like then we suffer, and if life does not progress in the way in which we would like, we suffer even then. In fact the Buddha taught that it is not the physical world which causes suffering, but our reaction to it. In other words, suffering is located in the mind, and in the reaction of the mind to the events around us. The New Kadampa Tradition emphasizes the continuity of the mind, and the fact that the mind is separate from the body. It argues that when we die the mind may be passed on to another existence. As a result it is important that we work hard according to Buddhist principles, since the mental delusions which we accumulate in one life may be passed on to another. This tradition places an emphasis upon trying to end this karmic transmission of delusion from one existence to another. One of the key ways to achieve this is through cultivating non-attachment. According to the New Kadampa we need to realize that becoming attached to the material world ultimately leads to suffering. Through meditation we should learn to become non-attached, and hence to have a more balanced and objective view of the world. The material world in all its forms is fundamentally impermanent. Everything which has a physical basis, including human beings, eventually dissipates and decays. This understanding of impermanence encourages a sense of compassion, since we become profoundly aware that as human beings we all share the same destiny. We thus develop the mind which is characterized by bodhicitta or a sense of compassion linked to a desire for enlightenment.

It is very difficult to abandon our sense of self, our sense of ego, and yet being able to do this is regarded as central to Buddhism. We are normally deeply attached to our concept of who we are; and also attached to many aspects of the physical world. However, when we truly understand the temporary nature of both ourselves and the world, we begin to understand the nature of what the New Kadampa Tradition refers to as emptiness. This means that there is nothing in the world to which we should become attached. We should let go of all the things which are dear to us. These might be close relatives, objects, feelings or anything to which we feel a strong sense of attachment. When we have truly let go of everything, we understand the nature of emptiness. There is nothing left to which we feel a bond of need or desire. At this point we have achieved enlightenment. We fully understand the nature of existence, and are no longer deceived by the appearance of the world.

Members of the New Kadampa are very much encouraged to develop compassion for other living creatures. However, it is not always easy to feel compassion for people. We do not necessarily feel compassionate towards those who are unpleasant to us and those who do not appear to share our opinions, and also towards those whose values appear to be different. On the other hand it is easier to feel compassion towards those who are kind to us, and towards those people who we like. Compassion arises when we become aware that we all share the same destiny in life. When we realize that all human beings to some extent share feelings of suffering, we tend to develop feelings of compassion.

Within the New Kadampa Tradition, the successful training of the mind is regarded as central to embarking on the path to enlightenment. It is felt to be very important to be able to maintain the stability and calmness of the mind, no matter what circumstances may arise. One of the features of our mind is that when it comes across objects or ideas, it tends to discriminate, either in favour of them, or against them. For example, when we are presented with a meal which is very plain and not very tasty, we tend to attach the label 'unattractive food' to it. On the other hand, if we are given some delicious food we attach the label 'attractive food'. In other words our minds discriminate in favour of whatever we think we would like to eat. Through meditation practice Buddhists try to train the mind to take a balanced view under all circumstances, and not to discriminate in favour of anything, however attractive.

Within Buddhism, a strong emphasis is placed upon the need for a teacher. It is very difficult with spiritual development to simply read scriptures or written accounts of teachings, and to make progress towards enlightenment in this way. We usually need to actually observe an experienced practitioner and to learn from observation how they put the dharma teachings into practice.

Social organization

The New Kadampa Tradition has over 1,000 centres based in nearly 40 countries around the world, which are dedicated to the teaching of Buddhist principles. They provide a range of courses for people at all levels of understanding of Buddhism. The New Kadampa movement has also established the International Temples Project which seeks to build temples around the world.

The movement has an extensive publishing programme based upon the writings of Geshe Kelsang Gyatso. Tharpa publications is the New Kadampa Tradition's own publishing company. The profits from these publications are passed on to the International Temples Project. The New Kadampa arranges international festivals when Gyatso himself teaches, and where meditation courses are offered. Geshe Gyatso first came to the United Kingdom in 1976 to teach at the Manjushri Institute at Conishead Priory, Ulverston, Cumbria, which ultimately was renamed the Manjushri Kadampa Meditation Centre. Gyatso later opened a new centre at York. Another temple was built at New York in 2005, and a further one is being constructed in Brazil. The organization has grown extremely rapidly. There have, however, been some residual doctrinal arguments that the organization is a new religious movement derived from the Gelug Buddhist School, rather than from the Kadampa tradition. Nevertheless, the organization continues to be very successful in attracting new members, and in providing a vehicle for the study of this Tibetan Buddhist tradition within a Western cultural milieu.

Ethical issues

The New Kadampa Tradition is apparently engaged in a mutual dispute with the Dalai Lama and his followers. The Kadampa movement worships a deity, Dorje Shugden, who is believed to protect the movement. The Dalai Lama, however, believes that Dorje Shugden has a rather negative influence, and has asked that this deity not be worshipped. This has led to conflict between some members of the Kadampa movement and some followers of the Dalai Lama. The Kadampa movement believes that Shugden is not evil. The deity is normally pictured holding a heart, symbolizing compassion, and although he has a fierce expression, this is supposed to represent his capacity to overcome delusion and inculcate wisdom.

Geshe Gyatso asserts that the deity has some of the qualities of the Buddha, and acts to protect the Buddha's teachings as exemplified in the movement. Whatever the rights and wrongs of this dispute, it arguably poses problems for the public image of Buddhism to have two related organizations arguing over this point of doctrine. In particular this is so, given the strength of feeling expressed in the dispute. It would arguably be a positive step for Buddhism if some amicable resolution could be found, especially given the virtues of compassion and tolerance manifested in Buddhism.

FURTHER READING

Bluck, R. (2006) *British Buddhism: Teachings, Practice and Development*, London: Routledge.
Gyatso, K. (1997) *Heart Jewel: The Essential Practices of Kadampa Buddhism*, London: Tharpa.

Heine, S. and Prebish, C. S. (2003) *Buddhism in the Modern World: Adaptations of an Ancient Tradition*, New York: Oxford University Press.

Sangharakshita (1991) *Facing Mount Kanchenjunga: An English Buddhist in the Eastern Himalayas*, Birmingham: Windhorse.

—(1997) *The Rainbow Road: From Tooting Broadway to Kalimpong – Memoirs of an English Buddhist*, Birmingham: Windhorse.

CHAPTER 6

SYNCRETISTIC MOVEMENTS

The religious movements discussed in this chapter are characterized by the way in which they have drawn upon different intellectual and religious traditions, in order to establish their teachings.
This is, in some ways, a feature of contemporary spiritual life, in
that through modern communications it is easier to acquire and
pass on information than it was in the past.

NEOPAGANISM

Establishment

The religious traditions and practices which existed prior to the
advent of Christianity were, as far as we can ascertain, very diverse.
They included concepts and ideas, particularly involving relationships between the divine and the natural world, which reflected a
complex and sophisticated view of the world. Historically, it often
seems that subsequent generations have failed to recognize entirely,
the true complexity of this world view, and have sometimes taken a
rather negative and indeed pejorative perspective on these religious
traditions.

This is reflected in the adoption of the term 'pagan' itself, used
for these pre-Christian traditions. When Christianity became
adopted as the state religion by the Roman Empire, previous religious practices gradually were disregarded and considered to be
primitive. They were, however, maintained to a considerable extent
in the country areas, while Christianity became the new religion
of the urban dwellers. The word pagan is derived from the Latin
'paganus', signifying someone who lives in a rural area. It is not

difficult to see how this word could gradually become associated with a simple and unsophisticated way of life. Gradually, it developed connotations of inferiority, of simplicity, and of a tradition which was unsuitable for a more advanced society.

It is reasonable to continue to employ the term pagan, although it is important to recognize the social context of its origins. The pagan religions are usually characterized by a close connection and empathy with nature. This manifested itself in such ways as the use of herbs in medicine. In medieval Europe these pagan traditions continued, but often had to do so secretly, since they were often regarded as a challenge to the prevalent, orthodox Christian society. There were many examples of the persecution of pagan groups such as witches, who would often have been perhaps practising herbalists, living in accord with ancient nature religions. Being so evidently different to the Christian norm, they would have been easily targeted as a subject for persecution. The word 'heathen' has also been used in much the same way as the term pagan to indicate someone outside the boundaries of the monotheistic, Abrahamic religions. Gradually, however, there developed a resurgence of interest in ancient cultures, particularly in the nineteenth century. Ancient patterns of polytheistic worship, and those focused upon the worship of a Mother Goddess, began to be seen as worthy of interest. Such approaches to spirituality also appeared to be in harmony with newer, developing conceptions of the importance of women in society, and the need to bring about reforms in the social status and equality of women. At the same time there was also an increasing interest in ancient myths, stories and legends, linked to pagan spirituality. There was a rather romantic vision of ancient legend which became more and more appealing. Equally, a growing sense of the importance of the natural world and eventually of environmentalism provided a renewed support for such nature-related spiritualities. In addition, studies of contemporary indigenous groups and societies such as the Inuit, indigenous Australians, and the tribal peoples of North America provided evidence of the sophistication of their belief systems. Spirituality appeared often to be completely integrated with their world view, so that all aspects of the world around them were considered sacred. This often contrasted with the view of religion in the West, where there was a clear distinction between the sacred and secular aspects of life.

Among some of the contemporary neopagan groups are Wicca, several different forms of nature worship, and druidism. Within these are a number of different traditions. Some are committed to trying to reconstruct the practices which existed in pre-Christian times, even though there is often a dearth of sources of information. Others accept that because of this, they may often have to develop new practices and rituals appropriate to contemporary times. Although there is great variety in neopagan movements, one tends to find some basic traditions which provide a sense of integration. There is often the concept of the Mother Goddess which provides a contrast to the male orientation of so many traditional religions, including those which developed in the Middle East. Some neopagan religions are also polytheistic, which, in a way comparable to Hindu traditions, may sometimes reflect a single deity or spiritual force which is seen as governing the universe. There is also very often a strong emphasis upon the significance of the natural world, whether or not this is actually worshipped as a form of divinity. These broad tendencies are found in Wicca, the British tradition of what is often loosely termed witchcraft. Wiccan ideas developed to maturity during the Bronze Age in Britain, with the building of long barrow burial mounds, and stone circles such as Stonehenge. When the European Celts began to invade Britain about 500 BCE, they adopted some Wiccan ideas even though these were not an intrinsic part of their culture.

Once Rome adopted Christianity in 312 CE, Wiccan traditions were gradually relegated to secondary importance, and were eventually only practised on the margins of society. Only after the Second World War, when specific legislation in Britain permitted the publication of material on Wicca, could the latter begin to take its place as a legitimate form of spiritual expression, recognizing finally some of the ancient traditions of England going back up to 5,000 years.

Teachings

Neopagans do not subscribe to any specific doctrinal system, partly because the roots of neopaganism have a number of different spiritual sources. One can, however, discern some commonalities in their teaching and world view. Very few neopagans, for example, believe in just a single God. This is largely because of their rather eclectic view of the natural world, where a spirit or deity may be associated with say a mountain, waterfall or tree, and where a number of Gods or Goddesses may be regarded as exercising control over the natural world. The cycle of the seasons is of particular significance, offering a structure around which many nature-related rituals occur. A major strand of neopaganism is that of the old Germanic and Norse religions which existed prior to the arrival of Christianity in Europe. Something of these spiritual traditions was recorded by Roman writers such as Julius Caesar during his records of the Gallic wars. There were a number of different deities in the ancient Norse pantheon, including Odin, the ruler of Valhalla, Thor, Freyja and Freyr, the deity of fertility. We have a record of some aspects of Norse religion and mythology in two Icelandic sagas named the Eddas. The original Norse and Germanic peoples seem to have had relatively little concept of an abode after death, although there is the relatively familiar tale of the dead warrior attaining Valhalla.

In Wicca on the other hand, there is rather more of a concept of life after death, although not as significantly as in Christianity. Many Wiccans have a belief in some form of reincarnation, for example, sometimes linked to the cyclical nature of their world view. For many Wiccans there is a belief in an all-powerful male God and an equally powerful female deity, which exist in union and possess equivalent power and authority. Some branches of Wicca worship the Mother Goddess exclusively. The male God is often symbolized as a horned creature and is perceived as a hunter, and also as a procreator.

The Druids were a cult of considerable significance in ancient Britain and Europe. The power of the Druids during the period of Roman Britain came from their religious authority, and their accepted right to organize sacrifices, and to be in authority in the courts. Julius Caesar, during his conquest of Gaul, studied the Druids, and mentions them in his treatise 'De Bello Gallico'. Druids were well-known for gathering among groves of trees which they declared sacred. Such trees were generally oak trees wherever possible, as mistletoe was valued for medicinal and other purposes. It was within such groves of oaks that Druids normally held their 'courts' and passed judgement in cases of disagreements between people.

Neopagans tend to perceive deities as both existing as spiritual realities within themselves, or as external spiritual realities. In other words, neopagans may think of themselves as having an element of the divine within them, while at the same time worshipping an external divinity. There is sometimes perceived to be an emphasis upon the Goddess, or female forms of deities within the neopagan movement, but this does not indicate any sense of emphasis on the female at the expense of the male. It is simply that there is an awareness of the tendency in many world religions to place a stress on male culture, and this goes some way to rectifying the imbalance. However, there are elements within the broad neopagan tradition, who worship only female deities. Neopaganism has a very strong commitment to various forms of nature worship, and its expansion since the 1960s can be related to the increasing and parallel concerns with the environment. Those concerned with protecting all aspects of our natural surroundings are often expressing in a secular way, the same sentiments which are expressed spiritually by neopagans.

Social organization

As a very broad principle, neopagans tend to be rather flexible about the organizational aspects of their faith, not feeling the need to adhere to strict doctrinal codes, and indeed feeling that dogmatism in religion can sometimes be counterproductive. Nevertheless, rituals, ceremonies and rites of passage are often employed to mark key events in the lives of neopagans, or to signify specific stages in spirituality. Magical ceremonies are often conducted, usually under the guidance of a spiritual teacher, in order to try to bring about a desirable end such as healing someone who is ill, or to enhance someone's spiritual understanding. In addition, much social and religious organization is structured around the cycles of nature, the seasons, and of the moon and planets.

At the festival of Imbolc on 2 February, neopagans celebrate the first signs of new growth in nature and the lengthening of the days. The first snowdrops appear, and may be used in religious ceremonies. By the festival of Beltane on 30 April, the plants, flowers and trees are growing, and people look forward to the fertility of summer. At the summer solstice or midsummer, people celebrate the culmination of the light and warmth of summer. As the days gradually shorten, and the produce of the land is gathered for winter, Samhain is celebrated on 31 October. This is also known as Hallowe'en, and is the festival at which the dead, and in particular deceased relatives, are remembered. Towards the end of December is the festival of Yule or the time of the winter solstice, the symbolic start of the New Year.

Neopagan traditions tend to require that new members pass through some form of initiation ceremony. It would not normally be sufficient to start simply taking part in meetings, but would require participating in a ceremony. In Wicca, a coven would normally be led by a high priest or priestess. Sometimes there would be joint leadership, although on other occasions, either one might take the role of leader. Such people in authority would normally conduct the initiation ceremony. Sometimes witches do not join together into a coven. A hedge witch is often a solitary witch, who may also practise certain skills such as being a herbalist. The word 'hedge' refers to the capacity to help people cross the 'hedge' or symbolic barrier, from the physical world to the world of the spirit. In neo-shamanism, the shaman also acts as an intermediary between the material and spirit worlds. The shaman assists others in communicating with the spirits of the other world. The shaman often has the capacity to immerse himself or herself in a trance-like activity, in order to achieve these spiritual goals.

Ethical issues

A considerable element in neopagan ethics derives from the commitment to nature and the environment. Neopagans therefore tend to be committed to moral principles which protect animal and plant life, which attempt to employ forms of energy which are renewable, and which employ resources, for example in the context of food, in a way which respects and renews the natural world. Many neopagans would thus grow as much of their own food as possible, and perhaps be more likely to be vegetarian than eating meat. Nevertheless it is also an important facet of neopagan ethics that they do not generally try to impose certain doctrinal values in others. As long as a particular belief or practice was not perceived to be harmful to others or to the environment, then they would not normally try to persuade others to change their ethical persuasion.

STUDY QUESTION

However, it is worth noting that many neopagans do believe in different versions of the concept of cause and effect in terms of ethics. In other words, they tend to believe that our actions taken today may well have moral consequences in the future. How might this moral principle be translated into attitudes towards nature and the environment?

As a general collection of different movements, neopagans aim for relationships which are non-dogmatic and which do not require people to adhere to religious norms. Equally well, neopagans generally avoid situations and organizations which are autocratic or have dictatorial leaders who try to impose certain values upon members of the organization.

Neopagans have very close feelings for nature and yet are not against technological advance. As a general principle they are not against technology, but do not feel it should be used simply for its own sake. It should be employed to enhance the state of the planet, rather than to cause a deterioration in the earth's ecosystem. However, tolerance is a major value system of neopagans who feel that they themselves should demonstrate a tolerant approach to belief systems and world views which are different to their own.

NEW AGE MOVEMENT

Establishment

The New Age Movement has no individual founder, nor any single scriptural or doctrinal basis. It has evolved rather than being founded, and yet despite the absence of a single founding figure, one can discern some early influences and precursors to the movement. It is reasonable to consider its inception as dating from the 1960s, when it was influenced by the broad movement of individualism, and rejection of established structures in society. There is a strong mystical trend in much of New Age thought, and one can argue that some of this at least derives from the late nineteenth century interest in Eastern religions such as Hinduism and Buddhism, and in broader, more general mystical movements such as Theosophy. However, as there is no definite point of establishment, and no specific set of beliefs to which members adhere, it is less easy to determine a precise intellectual or religious heritage for this new religious movement. The New Age Movement is by its very nature eclectic, and includes members and sub-groups with very diverse viewpoints. Nevertheless, despite the problems with providing a precise definition or set of criteria for membership, the concept of the New Age Movement is clearly understood in popular discourse, and the concept does have a meaning in the public consciousness. Thus, one can look to some key figures in the late nineteenth century, as having been at least influences upon the development of the movement, even though different commentators would no doubt suggest a different range of potential influences.

As suggested, one might point to the Theosophical movement and the writings of Helena Blavatsky (1831–91) as being an influence. This movement drew upon insights from a variety of spiritual influences, and in so doing had a sense of the factors which linked together all human beings. It was very much concerned with helping individual human beings achieve their full potential and develop spiritually, and in seeking to emphasize our shared humanity possessed a strong universalistic element to its philosophy. The Bengali poet, Rabindranath Tagore (1861–1941), and the French writer Romain Rolland (1866–1944) were both religious mystics, and very influential in the intellectual climate of the period. Other figures included George Gurdjieff (1866–1949) who drew widely upon ancient spiritual traditions in his writings and teaching, and Swami Vivekananda (1863–1902) who did a great deal to spread an understanding of yoga and Hindu mysticism in the West. Besides having a strong association with mysticism, and different forms of individual spiritual development, the New Age Movement has also tended to have a commitment to environmental and Green issues. In relation to this, both Mahatma Gandhi (1869–1948) and Leo Tolstoy (1828–1910) have probably been significant influences. During their lifetimes they corresponded with each other, and both established rural communes dedicated to a self-sufficient and non-exploitative lifestyle. They both advocated vegetarianism, a care for the environment, and in particular the philosophy of non-violence. Gandhi was particularly famous for employing the principle of non-violence as a form of political protest. He used it as a means of action against the British colonialists in India, and the manner in which he maintained a non-violent approach became an inspiration for the civil rights demonstrators in the United States, and indeed for non-violent demonstrations worldwide.

The term 'New Age' had been used in a variety of contexts before the movement became well-known in the 1960s. Generally, the term suggested the advent of a new era of peace, harmony and a more egalitarian lifestyle. In 1894 for example, the journal *The New Age*, much influenced by the Christian Socialist Movement was founded. It published articles on left-wing politics, the vote for women, literature, art, culture and spirituality. Between the years 1907–22 it became a very well-known journal under the editorship of Alfred Orage. Many leading authors of the period published articles in the journal including H. G. Wells, G. K. Chesterton, Katherine Mansfield, Arnold Bennett and G. B. Shaw. Just as it is difficult to determine the origins of the New Age movement with any certainty, it is also not easy, because of its eclectic nature, to define absolutely the teachings of this new religious movement.

Teachings

One of the most striking features of this movement is the emphasis upon the personal development of the individual. This is not a movement which seeks to encourage people to conform to clearly defined norms, but rather to embark on a journey of self-exploration. Such a journey may involve the development of the inner psyche, an understanding of the nature of the mind through meditation, the connection of the self with the cycle of life and death, the relationship of the individual with the earth, the planets, and the universe, and the development of new powers, such as telepathy. There is also an interest in the different facets of para-psychology, and in the establishment of psychic connections with beings in a different spiritual medium.

STUDY QUESTION

There is a generalized belief in the idea of a spiritual force which pervades the universe. This may be very like the Tao of Chinese religion. Such a spiritual force may be referred to as God, although the Judaeo-Christian connotations of this may encourage many New Age members to maintain their concept of the Divine on a more generalized level. Nevertheless, there is the broad idea that the universe is not a secular place, but that it is controlled and guided by a spiritual force with which we can interact. Besides Taoism, can you draw any similarities with other religious traditions?

The New Age movement has its own sense of ethics, for example, with regard to the notion of karma. There is a clear feeling that the karmic actions of today have consequences for our lives in the future, in a fashion similar to the notion of karma in Hinduism. This links very much with the concern with the environment which tends to be a significant element of New Age teaching. In particular, many New Age followers would probably subscribe to the Gaia hypothesis, or a variant of it, which essentially views the earth and its atmosphere as a self-contained biological system. This system is perceived as being normally in a state of dynamic equilibrium, such that it can adapt to any changes which disturb that equilibrium. The state of balance which has been achieved is assumed to be the optimal one for the organic life on the earth to be perpetuated.

The New Age movement tends to feel very positively towards the idea of holistic, naturalistic medicine. The use of herbal remedies, healing through the use of crystals, psychic healing, acupuncture, and the laying on of hands, are often considered to be appropriate forms of natural medicine. Different forms of meditation and yoga are also employed in these newer and more natural approaches to medicine. Many of the features of these natural remedies have probably been known for a long time. New Age followers do tend to have an affinity with ancient civilizations, and this manifests in a reverence for ancient sites such as Stonehenge and Glastonbury. Followers generally believe that such sites have a tangible presence of energy fields, a source of power which can be harnessed either for healing or for spiritual development.

New Age followers and organizations reflect a respect for feminine approaches to religion. They do not generally agree with the patriarchal traditions in many of the world's religious traditions, and indeed one finds women in positions of authority within the New Age movement. In addition, within New Age traditions which worship the Divine in various forms, one often finds a female deity or Goddess as the object of devotion.

New Age as a tradition arguably tends to have a stronger affiliation with Eastern religions than with the Judaeo-Christian religions of Judaism, Islam and Christianity. The reason for this may be that the latter faiths arguably place a greater premium upon adherence to scriptures and moral and religious norms than the former. Eastern religions, from Hinduism and Buddhism, to Shinto or Taoism, tend to concentrate upon the ideal of personal development, and the values of the religions are perhaps more subjective than preordained. This provides a looser, less-prescriptive context within which people can develop and define their own view of the world. The same principle applies to the many forms of self-development which are associated with Eastern religion, some of which have become a part of the secular, as well as spiritual element of society. Examples include hatha yoga, ayurvedic medicine and Tai Chi.

Social organization

In one sense, the New Age movement does not possess a social organization. There is certainly no hierarchy, with a leading authoritative figure at the head. It is not possible either to join this movement in the conventional sense. There is no formal membership, and no rites of passage. It would not be possible to produce a list of total membership, and followers of the movement would not need to state or subscribe officially to a belief system or creed.

Even though there is no overall membership, there are numerous small, autonomous groups or communities associated with the New Age movement. Such groups may be regarded as part of an informal network, in the sense that individuals may move between these communities to some extent, but these groups are not connected in any formal or official association.

A long-standing community, associated with many of the areas of interest of the New Age movement, is the Esalen Institute, at Big Sur, on the California coast. Since its establishment in 1962 it has developed a worldwide reputation in areas such as personal development, humanistic psychology, yoga, spirituality and meditation. The range of interests of the institute is very wide, and yet it does not appear to attach itself to a single discipline or category such as New Age. Nevertheless, its main interest areas seem very close to those normally defined as New Age. From its inception, it attracted renowned thinkers and writers such as Aldous Huxley, Carl Rogers, Paul Tillich and Alan Watts. The latter, a leading commentator and writer on Zen and Taoism, was a contributor to the Institute from the beginning. The Institute has sought to encourage new ways of exploring the spirituality of humanity, and new approaches to education and spiritual development. Among those who have given lectures at the Institute include Deepak Chopra and Carlos Castaneda.

Well-known venues for the New Age movement include Nimbin in New South Wales, Australia and Glastonbury in Somerset, England. Both have connections with alternative spirituality. The village of Nimbin is in an area which is regarded as spiritual by the indigenous Australians, and it is only since about the early 1970s that it has been adopted by the Australian New Age community, as a site for festivals and music venues. It attracted some notoriety as having a relatively relaxed attitude to the use of cannabis, although there were subsequently attempts to control this and enforce the law. Most types of New Age activity can be found in the area of Nimbin, and it is perhaps particularly known for its environmental initiatives.

As a historical and spiritual site, Glastonbury is often thought of in terms of the legends of King Arthur, and also the alleged association with Joseph of Arimathea and the Holy Grail. The blood of Jesus was claimed to have been caught in the Grail, which was later brought to England by Joseph. Arthur and Guinevere were said to have lived at or near Glastonbury, and it was once claimed that their place of burial had been located at Glastonbury Abbey. Glastonbury has been inhabited since prehistoric times, and these associations have made it a natural venue for New Age devotees. People come to Glastonbury for spiritual ceremonies on Glastonbury Tor, and also for the famous music festival, first held on a nearby farm in 1970.

It is probably true to say that the notion of a religious, spiritual or cultural organization, with clear role definitions, lines of responsibility and authority figures is anathema to the New Age movement. The social organization, if one can say it exists, consists in the knowledge of how people can contact each other, the location of key sites and events throughout the year, so that people can meet, and in the modern technological world, the techniques of computer interaction to share information and skills.

Ethical issues

There are a number of aspects of the belief system of the New Age movement which have an ethical dimension. Perhaps stemming from the belief that God is everywhere, or alternatively that everything in the universe is part of God, this then tends to encourage a respect and tolerance for other faiths. It is a reasonable assumption for New Age followers that all of the main religions of the world, lead to the same divine spirit or God. The different creeds of the world become simply different routes towards the same, identical goal. Such a philosophy discourages any form of discrimination or persecution, since we are all essentially working our way towards the same spiritual goal.

Equally, the very eclecticism of the New Age movement indicates an acceptance of a wide range of different religious viewpoints. This integration of different faiths and spiritual values within one movement produces a very inclusive world view which is accepting of virtually everyone, but on the other hand, it does render the movement somewhat difficult to define in terms of belief system. There is evidence here, however, of a significant ethical viewpoint, concerning a willingness to understand and accept multiple religious viewpoints.

Another important area within the New Age world view is their approach on environmental and green issues. The movement has done a lot to draw public attention to ecological questions, and continues to articulate concerns about the destruction of the environment. There are also connections here with the ethical systems of Eastern religions such as Hinduism and Buddhism, where the concept of ahimsa or non-violence is seen as very important. Ahimsa, as a concept, relates to all living things, including plants, and hence is relevant to the idea of caring for all aspects of the biosphere.

Finally it can be argued that the interest of the New Age movement in humanistic psychology, and the work of Carl Rogers and Abraham Maslow, has an ethical dimension. These psychologists discuss in particular the development by the individual of their full human potential so that in the fullness of their humanity they can, among other things, relate in a much more positive way with other human beings. Such 'self-actualization', as Maslow terms it, would appear to have parallels in the achievement of enlightenment in Buddhism. Achievement of such a mental state arguably enables people to act more ethically and in particular to work for the greater benefit and moral development of humanity.

HEAVEN'S GATE

Establishment

Heaven's Gate was a new religious movement which combined an interpretation of some Christian teachings, with a belief in

Unidentified Flying Objects [UFOs], and the landing of alien cultures from outer space on the earth. It was founded by Marshall H. Applewhite (1931–97) and Bonnie L. Nettles (1928–85). Applewhite was an able student, obtaining a Bachelor of Arts degree, and later becoming a music teacher, and university lecturer in music. Nettles was very interested in esoteric religion, was a member of the Theosophical Society, and it was probably she who influenced Applewhite to develop an interest in different aspects of spiritual thought.

Applewhite was probably gay, and seems to have had some relationships with male students at St Thomas University where he was a lecturer. This was at the beginning of the 1970s, and society was generally less tolerant about such issues than is now the case. Applewhite was asked to leave his post, an event which no doubt caused him much stress. He seems to have had difficulty understanding and adjusting to his sexuality, and it may have been during this period that he became attracted to the idea of celibacy. This later became a feature of the new religious movement which he founded. Applewhite met Nettles in 1972 in Texas, and they led a rather itinerant life in the United States for some months, discussing and developing their metaphysical theories. In broad terms they came to the conclusion that human beings were a less-advanced civilization than beings in outer space, and that Applewhite and Nettles had in effect been selected to die on earth, but to be transported via a UFO to join an alien civilization in outer space. Applewhite and Nettles used a number of pseudonyms during the existence of their group, for example, 'Bo' and 'Peep' respectively. They were also known as 'The Two' by the members of the group.

They lived in various parts of the United States, recruiting members with the claim that only their followers would be able to escape from earth to a better existence in outer space. Initially, they probably gained members numbering in several thousands, but many left, and only a tiny core of about 40 members were left at the end of the group. The Heaven's Gate group supported itself with donations from members, from one or two benefactors, and also from the income from a computer company founded by members. The movement was widely involved in the use of information technology, using it to recruit members, but also as a commercial enterprise. Their company was called 'Higher Source' and specialized in setting up websites for clients.

By the late 1990s, a view was beginning to develop that the only way to move rapidly to the more advanced level of development in outer space was to commit suicide. Applewhite argued that there was a UFO travelling with a comet near the earth, and the group should take the opportunity to join it. Some time in late March 1997, 39 members of the group including Applewhite committed suicide in California. When they were found on 26 March, all members were lying on their beds, in the same configuration, giving the impression that this had been a voluntary act.

Teachings

Applewhite and Nettles, influenced by the Book of Revelation, claimed that they had been sent down from Heaven, in order to facilitate the departure from earth of those who were prepared to join the more advanced society in space. Those who wished to achieve this had to join Heaven's Gate, and live according to the various teaching prescribed by Applewhite and Nettles. These teachings and lifestyle changes included a general renunciation of material possessions and a minimal level of contact with the outside world. Heaven's Gate members also lived a life of celibacy, and refrained from consuming alcohol. Generally speaking, the life style of the group could be described as one of asceticism and withdrawal from the world, a process which they believed would result in a total change in their psychology and physiology. This change was known as 'Human Individual Metamorphosis'.

Under Applewhite's influence the Heaven's Gate members believed that there was a distinct separation between the body and the human soul. The latter only adopted the body as providing a temporary residence before it moved on to a more sophisticated existence. This doctrine in effect laid the foundation for the teaching that suicide was the most appropriate way of gaining entry to the higher level of existence in Heaven. The human body was only perceived as a temporary place for the soul to exist, and hence it was of no real consequence when the body died. The movement believed that the planet earth was shortly to be restructured, and that it was essential for the group to escape at that juncture.

Social organization

The Heaven's Gate movement had a very simple and non-materialistic lifestyle. Generally speaking, they avoided as many examples of modern, materialistic living as possible. The lifestyle and culture of the group could reasonably be described as ascetic and monastic. Indeed the group members often used the terms 'brother' and 'sister' when addressing each other. When they first joined the group, they had given away many of their possessions and renounced contact with family members. The members adopted a celibate life, and this sexual asceticism was carried to such an extreme that Applewhite and seven other members of the group travelled to Mexico to undergo a castration operation.

The impression gained of the movement is that members were very disciplined in their behaviour, but that this was in a way, intrinsic to the members, rather than being a way of life imposed on them by an authoritarian leadership. In other words, one might argue that although their belief system and way of life could seem improbable and strange to many people, they would appear to have exercised a considerable amount of personal autonomy in believing and acting in the way that they did. The group did appear to have something of a complex about persecution, in that they believed that they might be attacked from without and prevented from continuing with their lifestyle. This may have been one factor in their deciding that the time had come to leave what they saw as their earthly existence, and to depart for existence on a higher plane. All members of the group, whether male or female, tended to wear the same uniform clothing.

Ethical issues

It appears that members of the group who had a crisis of confidence in the beliefs of the movement were asked to leave the group. In other words, they would not seem to have been coerced to remain, or attempts made to indoctrinate them into the group ideology. This does not point to the stereotypical image of a cult where people are under various forms of persuasion or are constrained in some way to remain as members.

Nevertheless, the history of this new religious movement does raise the serious question of what society should do, if anything, about minority religious groups with very unorthodox views. One might argue that as long as there is no coercion involved, they should be left to develop and live out their own ideas as they see fit. On the other hand, others might argue that society should either monitor such groups, and indeed intervene if necessary. These are difficult questions about individual freedoms, and the role of society.

THE CHURCH OF SCIENTOLOGY

Establishment

The Church of Scientology was established by L. Ron Hubbard (1911–86) in 1953. Hubbard was a successful writer of science fiction, but had eclectic interests in a number of fields, including religion. He was interested in finding ways to help people achieve their full potential, and to find their real selves, and as such developed initially the process known as Dianetics. As a young man he travelled widely, and was influenced by much of what he experienced, particularly the poverty and disadvantage which he saw. When he wrote his first book about Dianetics he could not have predicted the scale of its success. It did however become a best-seller. Initially, the process of Dianetics was designed to help people make the most of themselves, and to maximize their abilities. In the early 1950s Ron Hubbard began to develop his thinking on this subject, arguing that all human beings possessed an immortal spirit within themselves. Indeed he stressed that humans were fundamentally spiritual creatures. This evolution of Hubbard's thinking into the area of spirituality resulted subsequently in the development of the religion known as Scientology.

The pre-eminence of the spiritual nature of human beings resulted in Ron Hubbard reflecting on the nature of the soul. As he did not wish to cause any confusion with existing religions or existing use of the concept soul, Hubbard decided to employ the term thetan as a replacement for the more usual 'soul'. For Hubbard, the thetan is the very essence of the human individual – the most important aspect of the human being. It is a spiritual entity within the individual, which represents the creative force which drives the universe. Hubbard also argued that negative and disturbing experiences from the past become lodged in the mind as 'engrams', and these must be identified and their effects eradicated, before an individual can become a thetan. Scientology proposes a type of counselling known as 'auditing' which helps to counteract the effect of engrams, and ensure that the person achieves his or her true potential as a thetan.

During the 1950s various branches of the Church of Scientology were established in the United States. Hubbard spent the early years of the 1960s in England. In 1967 Ron Hubbard formed the 'Sea Organization' which was based on three ocean-going ships. The so-called Sea Org became an authoritative section within the Scientology movement. The latest additions to the teachings of scientology were often disseminated via the Sea Org. L. Ron Hubbard died in California in January 1986.

Teachings

According to the religion of Scientology, generally speaking, people try to act ethically and well towards their fellow human beings, but are often adversely affected by their life experiences in the past. These life experiences have an adverse effect on their spiritual development, their happiness and their behaviour. One of the key strategies of Scientology is to employ the help of an 'auditor' who will use the counselling procedures of 'auditing' in order to help the individual locate the source of the engram, or problem area in the mind. The auditor uses an E-meter, which measures small changes in the electrical resistance of the body. These changes in resistance are suggested to result from the location of the engrams. Using these techniques, the effect of the engram can be counteracted, and the persons begin to develop towards their potential. The ultimate goal of this new religious movement is to rid the entire world of the effects of these engrams, so that everyone can begin to achieve their potential.

This transition during which the engrams are eliminated is described as moving from a situation of 'pre-clear' to one of 'clear'. During the auditing process, the auditor asks a number of questions of the person in the pre-clear condition, in order to help them to rid themselves of the engrams. The questioning is conducted according to certain very precise rules. The auditor, for example, should not in any way express negative feelings about the responses of the pre-clear person. As the individual develops from a pre-clear condition to the clear condition, he or she is sometimes described as passing along the Bridge to Total Freedom. Eventually, when the effects of all engrams have been negated, the individual is described as becoming an 'operating thetan'.

The essence of scientology teaching is arguably that the most important element of the human being is the spirit, and that this spirit is connected to the universal spirit or God. Ron Hubbard was a prolific writer on Dianetics and on Scientology in general, and his writings are regarded by scientologists as the definitive analysis of the key concepts of the religion. Hubbard developed a range of precise concepts to use within the field of Scientology, and advocated their use as he felt that they would encourage more precise ways of thinking and analysing the ideas of Scientology.

Ron Hubbard's writings are held in great esteem within the Scientology religion and considered the basis of the teaching. It is generally not considered acceptable to discuss or reflect upon the teachings, as if they may be amended slightly. It is thought that the maximum benefit can only be gained from them, if they are used in their original, exact form. Equally, scientologists are committed to studying Hubbard's writings in a particular order, so that initially the less-complex concepts may be learned, followed by the more complex ideas. This sequential process is considered to be an important element in acquiring the knowledge and skills of Scientology. Importantly, the teachings of Scientology are regarded as being based upon empirical evidence. They are, therefore, regarded as having a firm theoretical basis, and indeed that their validity rests upon their capacity to improve the lives of those who adopt them.

Social organization

The main organization which teaches Scientology is the Church of Scientology International, which is based in Los Angeles. Each individual local church is a separate corporate body, with its own directors and chairperson. Until 1966 Ron Hubbard was in charge of the Church, but after that a great deal of the responsibility for the international church was assumed by a group of managers. There is a hierarchy of organizations and centres around the world, with large centres being the focus for a particular area. In 1959 Hubbard purchased Saint Hill Manor, in Sussex, England,

and this was the head office of the organization until the late 1970s. At about this time, the Church established major centres in the town of Clearwater in Florida, USA. A number of Scientology centres are also located in Los Angeles, including the publishing corporation which publishes the writings of Ron Hubbard, and also Scientology training organizations. The so-called Sea Organization dates from the time when Ron Hubbard acquired ocean-going ships as a location for running training courses and other Scientology-related activities. Members of the Sea Organization are generally recognized as among the more senior members of the Church of Scientology. Generally, the Church of Scientology has a hierarchical structure, and members are monitored in terms of their contribution to the Church. There are also organizations which concentrate on providing support for individuals who are experiencing difficulties. Criminon, for example, is an organization which exists to help prisoners, and to provide training which might help them restructure their lives. Narconon is a programme which helps those addicted to drugs. In addition, there are programmes developed by Hubbard, to help members with their education, but perhaps specifically with studying Scientology materials.

Ethical issues

The Church of Scientology has publicized extensively, the United Nations Declaration of Human Rights, in an attempt to do something practically to further human rights in the world. It has published leaflets on the subject, and also teaching materials for use in schools. In addition, scientology has opposed, for a long time, the use of psychiatry. In particular it has opposed the use of such strategies as electric shock treatment.

In Scientology terminology, the concept 'morals' is employed to refer to a set of principles which are normative in nature, and which create a set of parameters which define acceptable behaviour within the Sociology community. The concept 'ethics', on the other hand, is used to refer to a situation where someone is behaving in such a way as to have negative effects upon the Church of Scientology. In such a case, the Church tries to compensate for the effects of these actions, and also to encourage the individual to amend his behaviour.

FURTHER READING

Barner-Barry, C. (2005) *Contemporary Paganism: Minority Religions in a Majoritarian America*, New York: Palgrave Macmillan.

Harvey, G. (2007) *Listening People, Speaking Earth: Contemporary Paganism*, London: Hurst, 2nd edn.

Heelas, P. (1996) *The New Age Movement: Religion, Culture and Society in the Age of Postmodernity*, Oxford: Blackwell.

Hubbard, L. R. (1988) *Scientology: The Fundamentals of Thought*, Los Angeles: Bridge Publications.

Pike, S. M. (2004) *New Age and Neopagan Religions in America*, New York: Columbia University Press.

CHAPTER 7

A SYNTHESIS OF THE MAIN THEMES

This chapter examines some of the general themes and issues raised in our exploration of individual movements. We analyse, for example, issues concerning recruitment, culture, social isolation and change.

THE NATURE OF A NEW RELIGIOUS MOVEMENT

In any discussion of 'new religious movements' our attention inevitably turns to the three terms used in the title, and of these perhaps 'religious' is the most significant. When we choose to speak of an activity or an organization as religious, we probably, at least initially, base this upon our personal experiences of those enterprises which were introduced to us when we were young as 'religious'. For example, when reflecting upon whether an organization is religious, someone reared as a Christian would probably consider such things as a harvest festival service, Holy Communion, sermons, prayers to Jesus, the symbol of the cross and Christmas carols. They would probably ask themselves whether the organization in question had analogous objects, rituals and activities to those in the Christian church. Sometimes, however, a comparable list of activities may not be sufficient to establish the case that one is considering a religion. For example, a large business organization, or an education organization, may provide talks which are analogous to sermons; they will certainly have symbols, to represent their corporate identity, and they may have the equivalent of a 'hymn', for example, a school song.

Now Theravada Buddhism, for example, would appear to meet many of the above criteria as a religion. It has a symbol, for example, a statue of the Buddha in a meditation hall; it will usually participate in chanting extracts from the Pali scriptures, and it will have rituals such as the ordination of monks and nuns. However, unlike Christianity, Theravada Buddhism does not have any sense of communication with a metaphysical entity which exists beyond the material world. Christianity has a range of concepts including the existence of a single, all-powerful deity, and the intervention of that metaphysical entity on earth. Such ideas are absent in Theravada Buddhism. The purpose of Buddhism, as articulated by the Buddha, was the elimination of suffering; an enterprise which was to be achieved primarily by means of a careful sequence of practical activities, including meditation, which would appear to be principally psychological in character. The question thus arises whether Buddhism is a religion in the same sense as Christianity.

Such attempts at defining an organization as a religion rely upon the external application of apparently objective criteria, such as the existence of the concept of a God. However, there are other approaches to the general problem, and these include the application of what we might term 'internal' or 'intrinsic' criteria. This would involve analysing the impact on people of belonging to a so-called religious organization. For example, one might argue that people who belong to a religious organization have or develop an 'otherworldly' vision of the world. Although concerned with the practical matters of everyday life, they have a strong sense of the spiritual elements of life, of those aspects of life which reach out to something beyond the mundane and ordinary. Perhaps they have a notion of a sense of continuity beyond death, and a part of the individual human being which passes on in some way. It is in areas such as this that we perhaps find a shared vision between Theravada Buddhism and Christianity, for example. It is also within this type of perspective that one appreciates the spiritual and religious dimension of say, Scientology, with its concept of thetans (Kent, 1999). There are certainly some new religious movements which have unorthodox theologies and belief systems that to some would render them outside the parameters of a religious organization. Nevertheless, looked at from the point of view of their general spirituality, they may appear to be more significantly religious.

THE VARIETY OF NEW RELIGIOUS MOVEMENTS

One consequence of the expansion in the number of new religious movements has been the much wider choice of spiritual experience offered to people. There have been arguments that the general trend in Western society was one of secularization, an inexorable rejection of the religious dimension to life, in favour of a growing materialism. One could argue, however, that the wide range of new religious movements provides at least some evidence of a continuing need within society for religious experience. Moreover, this very multiplicity of religious movements also creates considerable competition between them (Swatos and Christiano, 1999, p. 222). New religious movements need financial backing in order to develop and grow, and this calls into question the various strategies employed by such movements to evangelize, to recruit new members, and then to retain their new membership. At the one extreme are movements which do not ask for contributions from members or the general public, and exist entirely on donations. At the other extreme are organizations which appear to put new members under varying degrees of coercion to contribute financially, and indeed to dispose of their assets in order to contribute more. In addition, some organizations use a number of strategies to make it very difficult for members to leave the movement. The Family International, for example, under its previous names of The Family, and The Children of God, would appear to have employed a variety of methods to ensure that some younger members did not leave the movement. When many religious movements developed during the 1960s, it was often relatively easy for them to recruit members from among the alternative society which developed at the time. However, as that generation grew older, and indeed had children themselves, those offspring were not necessarily as enthusiastic about life within a new religious movement as their parents had been. Many of these children had been reared within the environment of religious communes and centres. As they became teenagers they were more and more able to articulate their feelings about the organizations of which they found themselves members. In some cases, it is evident that such young people did not wish to replicate the lifestyle chosen by their parents. In the 1980s, for example, there is evidence that within the Family physical and psychological strategies were used to try to persuade such young people to stay; strategies which would not have been perceived as acceptable in the broader society (Kent and Hall, 2000).

In some cases, new religious movements find a ready source of members within immigrant communities. When people migrate to a new country, they often have difficulty in adjusting to the new values and culture. Slowly they can become disengaged from the values of their homeland, but at the same time find difficulty in accepting the way of life and the norms of their new home. Many such people join religious organizations. They may feel that such an organization provides an anchor point in their lives. They may feel somewhat lost in a state of spiritual and cultural uncertainty, and the firm values of a religious movement may enable them to orientate themselves better in their adopted country. For this to be successful, it helps if the religious value system of the movement they join is not dissimilar from that of their homeland. Ren (2007) carried out research into Chinese Christian Churches which have developed in California, and which cater particularly for immigrant Chinese communities. It was found that they 'tend to be strict and conservative and to insist on Biblical literalism' (p. 1). One might hypothesize here that the firmness of the theological teaching would be likely to find a ready ear among people who are seeking a sense of direction in a new and seemingly uncertain land.

RELIGIOUS MOVEMENTS AND CULTURE

New religious movements are very much dependent upon the cultural milieu in which they find themselves, or indeed seek to expand and grow. Their success or failure, or capacity to attract new members, often depends upon whether the social setting is conducive to such a development. In addition, in a situation where a new religious movement seeks to become in effect, a world movement, it is necessary for it to be sufficiently adaptable to meet the needs of different nationalities, different cultures and indigenous religions. If it is, for example, to attract new members from existing religions, then its theological position and teachings need to be able to absorb to some extent, the teachings of the existing religion. Unlike the previous example, in such a context, theological flexibility may be much more important than a very firm and strict ideology. Moreover, government policies increasingly differ in relation both to mainstream religion, and also to the development and tolerance of new religious movements. The movement needs to be able to evolve within a range of different governmental positions on new movements.

It has been argued by Nicolas (2007) that new religious movements can often be understood as flexible collections of belief systems integrated into a cohesive whole, but with the adaptability to
absorb members from a variety of backgrounds. In a study of the Sai
Baba movement it is argued that the organization has some appeal
to people from a wide variety of spiritual backgrounds, because of
this very flexibility. The study by Nicolas is of the Sai Baba movement as it has developed in Singapore, and it is pointed out that
the multicultural policy of the country has provided a sympathetic
environment for such a new religious movement to prosper. The
religious tolerance of the movement has also helped in its development, in that it 'teaches that all religions are equal, and oriented to
the notion of a universal God' (Nicolas, 2007, p. 6).

One of the major consequences of the proliferation of new religious movements has been, on the one hand, a degree of conflict.
This has taken place, not only between movements themselves,
somewhat suspicious perhaps of the intentions of other organizations, but also between new religious movements and the established, large-scale faiths. The latter have no doubt felt from time
to time, that the apparently unorthodox beliefs of many new religious movements represented a challenge to their more established
systems of spirituality. In addition, however, from a more positive
viewpoint, the variety of new religious movements has encouraged
no doubt, a greater degree of discussion about the plurality of belief
systems (Knott, 1993). On this positive note, Szerszynski (1992) has
described new religious movements as 'creative cultural experi-
ments' (p. 4). Their diversity has no doubt encouraged participants
to reflect widely on these newer forms of spiritual expression, and
to consider the form of spirituality which would be most suitable
for them.

RECRUITMENT

One of the major factors in attracting members to new religious
movements has been the sense of belonging to a close-knit, integrated group. In the postmodern world, social life is often characterized by fragmentation rather than solidarity. It may be something
of an exaggeration, but modern means of electronic communication tend to encourage socially isolated individuals to sit in front of
their computers, and to communicate with many other individuals

in a similar situation. People communicate with others on social networking sites and 'network' without necessarily getting to know each other well personally. Equally, the number of people who live on their own is increasing rapidly. There is a danger that this type of lifestyle leads to a situation of alienation from society. The new religious movement compensates for this, by providing a group with close social bonds, which nourishes a sense of belonging. Lewis (2000) has discussed this phenomenon in the context of Soka Gakkai International, the Mahayana Buddhist group which originated in Japan.

New religious movements are also often attractive to new members because of the dramatic improvements in lifestyle which they offer. This transition often offers a change of life which is only accessible to a select minority of a particular movement. Holden (2002) discussed such a transition in relation to the Jehovah's Witnesses movement. He notes that the Jehovah's Witnesses 'propound an exclusive millenarian theology' (p. 2) which argues that only a minority of members will ultimately gain access to Heaven. To some this may seem an improbable assertion and promise, while to others it may be an extremely attractive proposition. New religious movements, as a general rule, do tend to offer a change of life which can be very attractive. They invite people to leave behind their previous life with all of its perceived imperfections, and to adopt a new lifestyle, which promises various advantages ranging from entry to the Kingdom of Heaven to perhaps a comforting fraternity and social support mechanisms.

One of the abiding, and sometimes notorious, aspects of new religious movements is that they are often founded, developed and controlled by a leader with considerable charisma. Indeed, it may be difficult to imagine a religious movement as being founded in any other way. On the positive side, a charismatic leader can provide vision, inspiration, leadership, knowledge, and spiritual and religious teaching. On the negative side, members of the religious movement may find a charismatic leader too controlling and dictatorial. Such a leader may define too precisely the norms, values and beliefs of the group. Nevertheless, a strong set of values, whether consisting of religious doctrine or of moral injunctions, may be very attractive to a potential member. As we have argued above, fragmentation of knowledge and values is a feature of postmodern society, and although this provides flexibility for people to choose their own world view, it may also leave people in a kind of spiritual or ethical vacuum. The sheer variety of belief systems may make it very difficult for people to decide on a personal value system. Thus, the idea that they could join a movement with a very specific set of beliefs and ways of behaving may be very attractive, and may indeed be an active recruiting tool for the religious movement. This can provide certainty in a world of uncertainties. It can provide a set of rules to live by, when there do not appear to be any rules; or perhaps, the rules are too numerous and diverse. In the case of many new religious movements, when the original charismatic leader retires or dies, there is a gradual transition to a more bureaucratic structure, where the personal charisma of a leader is of less consequence. This pattern of development is discussed by Chryssides (2001).

In addition to the influence of a charismatic or persuasive leader, it is sometimes argued that new religious movements employ a range of strategies in order either to win new converts, or to keep them as members once they have joined. For example, a charismatic leader may develop a range of norms of behaviour, rituals and conventions, with which new members of the movement are required to comply. In this way, there is consistency of approach throughout the movement. There are, however, two different ways of looking at such a practice. On the one hand, it can be viewed as unduly oppressive and manipulative to insist on certain patterns of behaviour; on the other hand, it might be viewed as providing a sense of stability, which will provide members with a sense of belonging.

STUDY QUESTION

It is perhaps worth bearing in mind that new religious movements exhibit a wide plurality in their customs and approaches. There is no one consistent approach to the recruitment of new members, or to the treatment of existing members. Equally, people will react very differently to the same customs or communal practices. Some will be offended and annoyed by an apparent loss of liberty and autonomy, while others will feel perfectly happy within a very structured framework. Are there any criteria we can apply to decide whether people are being treated inappropriately?

It is, therefore, extremely difficult to generalize in terms of new religious movements. Some would argue, for example, that when someone first joins a new religious movement, they are often required to adhere to a particular pattern of behaviour, and to accept specific customs and norms which have been established for the group. To some extent this is the same for anyone who joins a new social group. When one starts a new job, for example, there follows a period of socialization in which one gradually becomes accustomed to certain ways of doing things. In some occupations this process may be regarded as acquiring 'professional values' and gradually appreciating how that particular professional has come to treat its clients or customers. This is not usually problematic within an occupational group, because those values and practices are within the public domain. They are even sometimes recorded in the form of a professional code of practice. The way in which professionals are required to act is often within the scope of common knowledge, and hence is a reasonable expectation of clients of that profession. There is no reason why religious groups should not act in the same way, to the extent that they treat new members in a certain way, and according to certain standards which are clear and can be placed in the public domain. Many established religions in fact do this, for example, in the context of trainees submitting themselves for training for ordination, or in the context of novice monks and nuns. Usually, the trainees know exactly the nature of the process they will experience during their period of induction.

The crucial feature of such processes, however, is that normally they are transparent, understood by all parties beforehand, and importantly, if the trainee decides that they are not happy with the process, then they may easily disengage without there being any undesirable penalties or consequences. When criticisms have been voiced about new religious movements in terms of their induction of new members, it has usually been because some of the above features have not allegedly been as open or transparent. It has been suggested, for example, that the requirement for new members to conform to the values of the group has been used in some contexts, as much to control the individual as to ensure a system of shared values. One can understand that a new religious movement, or indeed any religion, needs to have some commonality of values and beliefs, since otherwise the purposes and religious beliefs of the group would not be clear. When people join a religious movement they need to know what they are joining! It is equally reasonable to suppose that new members should try to adhere to these beliefs and principles in order to ensure the cohesion and coherence of the group. However, it has sometimes been claimed that some movements have employed unacceptable methods to try to ensure the compliance of newcomers, and that such methods have unnecessarily and unethically manipulated those new to the movement.

When someone takes the decision to join a new religious movement, it is often a decision to which they have given considerable thought, and they hence wish to make a success of it. They want to be accepted within the group, and also to win the approval of the longer-serving and most senior members. To that extent it is not very different to someone starting a new job. Therefore, it is possible for the leaders of the movement to exert influence over new members, simply because the latter are often so eager to be accepted. New members want to learn the correct rituals, learn elements of the scriptures if this is relevant, and generally make friends among the members of the movement. It is possible for the leaders of the movement to criticize new members, to suggest that they are not trying sufficiently hard to integrate themselves within the group, or to suggest that they are still retaining the values of people who are outside the movement. They may suggest that new members have not sufficiently abandoned the values of their previous lifestyle. The latter can be a particularly powerful argument where the religious movement claims that its ethical values are different and more valid, when compared to those of the wider society. A failure to meet those ethical values on the part of a new member may be used as a criticism of the new member's approach to the movement.

SOCIAL ISOLATION

In order to strengthen such an argument, new members may be exhorted to abandon contact with aspects of their previous lives. They may be asked or told to sever contact with previous friends and with family members. One of the effects of this is that they then have no means of comparing their new value system with their previous one. They cannot phone someone, and discuss their new lifestyle or its values. This means that they do not have any possibility of discussing different views or of critiquing their new value system in any way. Clearly, they will be able to remember how they would have responded previously to situations, but slowly memories will fade, and such memories will be replaced by a single world view or ideology – that of the new movement to which they belong. The values of the new religious movement will become their sole reference point, and gradually they may come to regard it as the only perspective upon reality.

In the more extreme cases a movement may develop rules which limit any possibility of communication with relatives and previous friends. The movement may live in a physically isolated environment, and may limit the way in which any communication can be made. For example, it may not be permitted for members to have mobile phones, and there may not be any other method of telephoning. Such measures may be justified to new members on the grounds of the need for uninterrupted spiritual practice or meditation, but the end result is a closed society, where the novice member becomes more and more under the control of the organization. Various rules may be introduced which ensure that members remain physically within the confines of the organization, much in the same way that an enclosed order of monks and nuns may be permitted very few visits to the outside world.

Gradually, the religious movement may become the only world known by the members, and it becomes more and more difficult to sever contact with it, and leave the organization. Particularly this is so in a situation where new members are encouraged to part with financial and other assets before they join the movement. Even more so, there may be situations in which a condition is placed upon new members to make donations of their financial assets to the organization. In such cases, it may then become impractical for someone to leave the movement, as they are then both psychologically and materially dependent upon it. The control which may be exerted under such situations is probably greater than is so with a secular organization, even one such as the armed forces. In the latter case, there will be a written contractual arrangement which is in the public domain, and far from demanding that the individual contributes financially to the organization, the latter pays the individual. In addition, even though in the case of the armed forces, the new recruit wishes to obtain the approval of the commanders, the limits of what he or she may be asked to do are clearly specified and understood.

This discussion is not to suggest that all or even the majority of new religious movements adopt such measures from the perspective of trying to control and manipulate its members. Some movements may adopt them to a certain extent, from the purely innocent perspective of trying to create an atmosphere in which spiritual practice may flourish. There is, however, in all such situations, an overriding ethical requirement known as informed consent. This principle argues that before someone is asked to do something, or asked to join an organization or to participate in an activity, they should be as fully informed as possible. They should fully understand the consequences for themselves, and the way in which they will be treated. It is only if they are operating from a position of complete knowledge and understanding, that they can make a truly informed choice. Not to have that knowledge and understanding removes something of a person's autonomy as a human being.

In the case of a new religious movement it is particularly important from an ethical point of view that people retain their autonomy of action, because it is very easy for people to submit to a belief system. If they feel that a belief system will give meaning to their lives, and help them make sense of the world, then they will sometimes, in their enthusiasm, be willing to hand over their sense of free will and autonomy to an organization. In such a situation it behoves the organization to act responsibly and to ensure that the genuine freedom of action of the individual is maintained. It is in this area of the recruitment of new members, and the manner in which they are subsequently treated, that there has been some contention. In discussing these issues two well-known studies are Barker (1984) and Singer and Lalich (1995).

CHANGE AND TRANSITION

One feature of new religious movements which can be disconcerting to members of established faiths is their radicalism. By their nature they do tend to challenge traditional belief systems, and to present often, extremely different ways of looking at the world. One can argue that this is particularly so with those new movements in which the natural world occupies a central position. In premodern times, at least in the religions of the near East, the natural world was seen as the creation of a single, all-powerful God. The possibility of the perfection of human beings was seen as the main theological concern, rather than any thoughts about the natural world. The latter, when it was considered, was seen as a context within which human beings could strive to fulfil the will of God.

The centrality of human beings in their struggle for spiritual perfection was replaced in the modern period with a concern for the
domination of nature through the use of science and technology.
Human beings remained as the central consideration, but there was
a growing belief that they had the potential to control the natural
world by means of their intellects. In the premodern period there
was little understanding of the mechanisms of the world, and of
the way in which the different elements of the natural world could
be conceived as an integrated whole, linked by the principles of the
physical and biological sciences. The functioning of the world was
seen as the province of God. As our understanding of these scientific, rational principles increased, some started to consider that
it might be possible to explain and understand the world entirely
through the mechanisms of science, and that the concept of the
intervention of God was becoming redundant. Nature was again
relegated to a secondary position, but in this case to the new-found
power of science and technology. There was a growing belief that
it was possible to control nature and to use its powers for the benefit of humanity. As we now know to our cost, the notion that one
could exploit nature for the selfish benefit of mankind, without any
adverse consequences, was a mistaken one.

As we move into the postmodern period, there is first of all a
realization that concerns for the environment should be central to
plans for the development of humanity. In addition, the advent of
computer technology in the postmodern period and the expansion
of electronic communication have resulted in a great increase in the
dissemination of knowledge. As people have gained access to more
and more information, it has opened up the possibility of many new
ways of viewing the world, including new ways of understanding
spirituality. One could employ this line of reasoning in helping us
to understand the expansion of new religious movements, and in
particular of those which place a spirituality of nature as central to
their concerns.

In the postmodern, computer-based world human beings have
the potential to make connections between a wide range of ways
of viewing spirituality, and to construct and re-construct new concepts of themselves in a religious sense. They have the potential now
to declare that they will now view and interpret their spirituality in
a certain way which perhaps did not exist before. Sometimes this
might involve the adaptation of a pre-existing spiritual form, and

on other occasions the creation of a completely new spiritual vision of the world. This appears to be particularly so in relation to those new religious movements such as neopaganism, neoshamanism, New Age and Wicca, which involve placing the natural world at the centre of their religious cosmos. As York (2000) argues, one might view such new religions as a 'protest movement' which 'questions or challenges a dominant position' (p. 3). It is in fact, a major transition to move from a position of exploiting nature, and of finding new ways of using its raw materials, to seeing nature as an essentially spiritual entity, which we can draw upon for spiritual sustenance. This is a radical transition, and not one which some people would find easy to make.

The concept of nature as a source of spirituality is not, however, a new idea. It is fundamental to Eastern religions such as Taoism and Shinto, and permeates many aspects of Buddhism and Hinduism. The concept of ahimsa, or non-violence in Hinduism, relates as much to non-violence to the natural world, as to non-violence to other human beings. The ideas of these faiths are drawn upon by new movements such as New Age, and continue to provide a source of inspiration for new ways of expressing contemporary spirituality.

FURTHER READING

Barker, E. (ed.) (1982) *New Religious Movements: A Perspective for Understanding Society*, Lewiston: Edwin Mellen.

Cowan, D. E. and Bromley, D. G. (2008) *Cults and New Religions: A Brief History*, London: Blackwell.

Dawson, L. L. (ed.) (2004) *Cults and New Religious Movements: A Reader*, Oxford: Blackwell.

Lewis, J. R. (2003) *Legitimating New Religions*, New Brunswick: Rutgers University Press.

Miller, T. (1995) *America's Alternative Religions*, Albany: State University of New York Press.

PART III

SOCIOLOGICAL AND PSYCHOLOGICAL THEMES IN NEW RELIGIOUS MOVEMENTS

CHAPTER 8

PSYCHOLOGICAL THEMES IN NEW RELIGIOUS MOVEMENTS

The nature of new religious movements raises a number of issues which have a distinctively psychological orientation. There are the variety of motivational factors which induce people to join religious movements, and the psychological interactions within a fairly 'closed' society of the leadership, existing members and newcomers. There is also the question of whether members of new religious movements are generally able to exercise their free will and autonomy in group situations. This chapter examines such issues.

THE INDIVIDUAL SEARCH FOR SPIRITUALITY

People are motivated to join new religious movements for a variety of reasons, but one significant factor can be the feeling that other religious systems are unsatisfactory to them for various reasons, and that they hope to find a world view which meets their specific needs. They, therefore, hope to find a movement which is sufficiently different to make them feel that they have found something which, if not unique, is distinct enough to provide them with their personal credo. There may also be a slightly egoistic element here, in that some people are motivated by the desire to be different to others, to feel that they have found a spiritual path that others have missed.

It perhaps follows from this that if new religious movements are to appeal to this psychological tendency in some people, then they need to establish ways in which they are different and distinct from other religious movements. Religions have always tended to do this, and indeed if they had not done so, they would probably not have persisted as individual belief systems. In the most unfortunate of circumstances, this tendency to establish distinct belief systems has led to serious conflict between groups, as they each attempted to establish their validity in terms of religious truth. However, in a sense, there is a fine line to draw in terms of establishing a group's individuality. If a religious movement develops a theology or belief system which is too unusual, then it may only attract a small group of members. On the other hand, if the movement is fairly similar to other groups, then there is no real motivation for people to join. The movement needs, in a sense, to be sufficiently different to appeal to new members, but not so different that it appears excessively eccentric and therefore off-putting to people. The Aetherius Society, for example, with its belief in communication with an extraterrestrial form of intelligence, is relatively unusual in its belief system, and attracts only a small membership when compared with other movements. On the other hand, the Rajneesh movement brought together in its teachings a range of ideas from different sources, and some unique to the organization itself. It did, however, attract a great many members, perhaps partly through the charisma of Rajneesh or Osho himself, but also because of the teachings and organization. The forms of meditation developed by Osho were different, but still recognizable as meditation, and this coupled with aspects of the teaching and social organization made the movement at its height, very fashionable.

One aspect of a new religious movement that can render it very attractive to potential members is when it claims to provide benefits only to those who join as members and comply with its teachings. Members then feel that they are obtaining something very special, and particularly this is so if the movement links itself to the possibility that members can gain salvation for their soul, or be spiritually liberated or enlightened in some way. If members can be persuaded of the veracity of such a claim, then such teachings can result in a very strong commitment to the movement. Members are very reluctant to leave the movement, as they feel they will lose the possibility of salvation. The justification for such claims often derives from the analysis of scripture. This can be a stronger form of justification than simply a claim by a charismatic leader. Verses from religious texts can often be interpreted and then re-interpreted to act as 'evidence' for particular truth claims, when in fact such verses may be subject to multiple possible interpretations. The leader of a movement can point to something as tangible as a text, when trying to support assertions. Such claims are often linked to the idea that the scripture or holy book represents the word of God. The allegedly divine nature of the holy text coupled with an interpretation which apparently supports the unique nature of the new religious movement may together constitute a forceful argument in favour of the belief system of the movement.

The psychological impact of such ideas upon members may be reinforced by additional claims by the leadership of the movement that in order to fully appreciate the implications of the scriptural verses, the member of the movement must undergo a period of intense training. This kind of argument generates a type of exclusivity to the teaching, so that those who have undergone the additional training become a type of elite within the movement. They then feel they are privy to specialized training which provides them with feelings of authority and power over the 'ordinary' members of the group. On occasions, some movements require payment for such teaching, and this payment may often be quite substantial.

ECONOMIC ISSUES IN NEW RELIGIOUS MOVEMENTS

The issue of finance in new religious movements is a sensitive one. It is clear that any organization requires some money in order to function. The principal issue for an organization is not the need for money, but the way in which that money is raised, and the amount of money solicited. This is particularly important for a religious organization where there are expectations that it will act ethically simply by virtue of the fact that it is a religious organization. Some new movements have membership fees or ask for payment for courses and the accompanying residential costs. All of this may seem acceptable if it is kept within reasonable bounds. Some organizations do not charge people for courses or training if they are unemployed or retired. There is perhaps an issue about the charging of fees for religious teaching. Some may argue that there is a difference between charging fees for art classes, university courses or vocational courses and asking for payment for the kind of spiritual teaching which takes place in a religious organization. Some might argue that because religious teaching is concerned with helping people to lead a more fulfilled life, and perhaps in consequence to be able to help others in their turn, it is ethically wrong to charge money for this. However, this is a difficult issue, since others might argue that there are similar elements present in educational courses.

STUDY QUESTION

A much more contentious area concerns the request or demand that new members of religious movements sign over major assets such as houses or investments to the movement. This may be even more contentious where it is suggested that those who make major donations will have access to a more prestigious position in the organization or to a leadership elite. What are your views about a situation such as this?

In a psychological sense, quite apart from in a moral or financial sense, such practices may be problematic. It might be argued that movements which make such demands are taking advantage of the psychological needs of some people to be accepted within a group. The members are, in effect, purchasing a degree of social acceptance. They are being offered apparent social status and acceptance in exchange for substantial sums of money or assets. Perhaps even more concerning is the psychological dependence which can arise, simply because the individual becomes financially dependent upon the religious movement. For those who have handed over a substantial part of their assets, it will be much more difficult to leave the organization if they wish to do so in the future. They will be dependent on the movement for their food and shelter, besides the psychological support of members. It may be morally acceptable for someone to hand over assets if one does this from a position of informed consent and complete autonomy, but not if there is a degree of coercion, or if there is an implied gaining of social benefits. It also behoves the leadership of organizations to make the purposes of donations clear and transparent. Financial contributions should be used for specific purposes which are clear to the donors, rather than simply accumulating in bank accounts which are at the disposal of an elite group within the organization.

PREPARING FOR GREAT EVENTS

In some movements, elite groups may be entrusted with the organization of a period during which the movement prepares for the coming of an expected spiritual teacher, messiah, religious leader or guru. This is particularly so within so-called millenarian groups, which suggest that there will be a 1,000-year period, the millennium, during which the movement will prepare for the advent of the new spiritual leader. Once the leader arrives, there will be a continual period of peace, happiness and salvation, but usually only for a select group from the movement. In some Hindu-oriented groups there are claims that the teachings of a guru or spiritual leader can enable members of the movement to attain moksha or liberation from the unending cycle of birth and death.

In contemporary times, it is not too difficult for movements to predict that either a natural disaster or indeed some form of persecution will have a disastrous effect upon a religious movement. From a psychological point of view, the threat of persecution or annihilation may help the group to bond together and act as a cohesive whole. It may strengthen the collectivity, and give the movement a feeling that it must act together in order to survive. If the leader of the movement offers a line of action to help preserve the group's identity, then it may strengthen the leadership and enhance the loyalty of members to those in authority.

If, at the same time, the leader of the movement claims that the strategy is a completely novel one, and that it has never been employed before within the movement, then this may be attractive to members. It may improve the way in which the leader is viewed, and give him or her a fresh sense of authority. Members of the group may develop the feeling that the group is moving in a fresh direction, that they have found a new sense of motivation, and that the movement has found a new lease of life.

There are many people in the world who may have anxieties and feel pressures upon them, and it would be all too easy for an organization to play upon those fears in order either to recruit them or to persuade them to remain within an organization. If a new religious movement were to argue that some form of disaster was imminent, then such predictions could increase the anxiety felt by some people. The basic moral premise here is that it is unacceptable to take advantage in any way of those who are anxious or psychologically dependent. As Rambo (1998, p. 3) argues, 'no religious group should seek to exploit the vulnerable, whoever they are'. It would seem reasonable to argue here that when a religious movement, or any organization for that matter, helps people who are psychologically

NEW RELIGIOUS MOVEMENTS: A GUIDE FOR THE PERPLEXED

dependent in some way, then that help should be unconditional. The help should not be provided with a view to gaining something in return from the person.

Psychological dependence in people may also be generated by claims made by new religious movements. Such claims may be of various types, but an example is the making of predictions which could apparently be of great benefit to members of movements. The doctrine of the 'second coming' of Jesus, for example, is found in a number of different movements, and predicts the return of Jesus to earth, along with the associated salvation of certain groups of individuals. Some movements have made associated predictions about the actual date on which such events will happen. Such predictions tend to generate great excitement and anticipation within a movement, and often have the effect of creating a strong sense of group solidarity. Members are linked together by the feeling that they are sharing in the experience of a great event. There is also perhaps the sensation that because they are members of a particular movement which will share in this experience, they are also 'special' and different from the rest of society.

If, however, the prediction fails to materialize on the stated day, this can lead to a great deal of disappointment and uncertainty within the group. Various strategies may be employed to account for such a failed prediction. It may be argued that the basis of the prediction had been misinterpreted. For example, if the prediction had been based upon religious texts, it may be suggested that the texts should have been interpreted in a different way. The prediction may be amended to some new date in the future, based upon a revised interpretation of the data. Alternatively, it may be argued that the social circumstances were not appropriate for the event to happen. It may be suggested that the members of the movement had failed in some way to be receptive to the particular event. In effect this places the 'blame' for the failed prediction on the members of the movement.

When a prediction fails to materialize, there is clearly a tendency for members of the movement to be disillusioned and even to leave the movement. Some members may feel that the movement has failed them, and they therefore abandon the movement and its teachings. In other cases, they may be persuaded that a revised prediction will eventually occur, and therefore wait for this to happen. In other cases, they may be persuaded that the failed prediction relates in some way to an inadequacy on the part of the members, and that they should simply try harder and be more committed in the future. This might involve more prayer, or devotion to ritual, and more serious and committed adherence to teachings. If it happens that new predictions fail, then there is perhaps a limit to which members may be prepared to remain within the organization. In some cases, a religious movement retains the idea of a prediction as part of their teachings, but places no specific time or date on the occurrence of the event. The Seventh-day Adventist Church, for example, predicts the second coming of Jesus Christ, but regards this as likely to happen at any time. In other words, members of the Church must always be prepared for this to happen.

DEPENDENCE

The great advantage of a religious prediction from a psychological point of view is that it can give considerable hope to people, in a world which may at times seem devoid of hope. Among those who share in that vision of hope, it can create a strong sense of group solidarity, in that everyone feels united by that same vision. On the other hand, because it encourages people in a sense to submit to the idea of the prediction, it can initiate a sense of psychological dependency. It can also result in a loss of some degree of personal autonomy, since the individual becomes so dependent upon the outcome of the prediction. Walsh and Bor (1996) have conducted research upon the nature of dependency within new religious movements, and in a celebrated study Festinger, Riecken and Schachter (2008) explored the nature of prophecy within a religious movement which claimed to be in contact with extraterrestrial intelligence.

One of the interesting psychological features of new religious movements is the all-embracing enthusiasm and commitment often shown by members. It often appears that members of such groups find it difficult to be a member and yet to continue a balanced social and work life. They often appear to embrace their new-found group membership, and to abandon many or all aspects of their previous lives. Why thy feel able to do this, or indeed want to do it, is not easy to understand. It may be that by their nature, some people who join new movements are intrinsically insecure or unhappy about their lives. When they find a group and belief system to which they feel attracted, it may provide them with an entirely new focus for their lives. They, therefore, may take little persuasion in abandoning their previous existence. As part of this psychological state they may also become too dependent upon the leaders or teachers of the group. They may assume that the leader really does have a total and comprehensive view of reality, and that this world view will provide answers to all the questions which they had. They may, in effect, stop questioning the leader, and simply accept his or her pronouncements. Some may be happy with this situation, and not feel the need to exercise their own autonomy. In fact they may feel that the movement is correct in an absolute sense, and that therefore any challenge to their ideas is misplaced. On the other hand, some people may reach a point where they begin to lose confidence in the movement's teachings, and it is at this point that they may consider leaving. The complexities of life within a new religious movement, and the tensions between having faith in the movement and yet exercising one's own autonomy are revealed in the study by Downing (2001) of the San Francisco Zen Centre. It should be noted here perhaps, that while Zen Buddhism is clearly not a new religious movement, its establishment in the West, in a different cultural milieu to Japan, appears to create at least some nuances of the psychology of a new religious movement.

NEW RELIGIOUS MOVEMENTS AND CHILDREN

Among all the discussion about new religious movements and the psychological issues which are raised about life in a religious community, it is easy to forget the potential effects upon the children and young people who are brought up within such a society. The seemingly obvious point to make is that when their parents join a new religious movement, particularly if they choose to live in a communal environment, their children do not have any choice. They cannot exercise their personal autonomy and choose to live in a different environment. An interesting account, in this regard, is that of Guest (2005) who describes his childhood within the Rajneesh community. It is perhaps worth reflecting that adults who join a religious community have experienced previous lifestyles with which they can make a comparison. If they choose to join a new religious movement, they have the opportunity to exercise their rationality, and decide whether it is appropriate for them. They can again choose to exercise their rationality and leave the movement if they wish. Their children, on the other hand, do not have these choices. When they are reared within a religious movement with a single ideological perspective, then they have to try to understand the world within that viewpoint. They are not able to make comparisons and to slowly formulate their own philosophy of the world. This is not to say that many children brought up within religious communities do not become balanced, well-adjusted adults, but the psychological development of children brought up in such circumstances remains an important question.

THE CLOSED SOCIETY OF A NEW RELIGIOUS MOVEMENT

For those who are living within a new religious movement, within the parameters of the prevalent ideology, the belief system may seem completely natural and consistent, yet to outsiders their beliefs may appear nonsensical. As Heelas (1996, p. 3) has pointed out, this phenomenon does require some explanation. Within mainstream society, it can be argued that there is constant interaction between individuals. This occurs on a micro-level through conversation, emails and letters, for example. It is through this constant process of interaction that we propose ideas to others, and in exchange receive their opinions. This is a form of negotiation between individual members of society, as to which forms of belief system are acceptable. If a small group of people feel strongly about an issue, and mount a small demonstration, others may think that they have a good idea and join the group. Their ideas may spread and gather momentum. On the other hand, there may be a feeling that the idea is silly, in which case it will probably gradually disappear except perhaps for a small band of supporters.

This happens at all levels of society, from the level of individual citizens right up to the level of government. If the latter should propose a new policy, it will either be generally accepted by the electorate, or there may be a hue and cry against it. In the latter case, governments may sometimes change their view and amend their policy. This overall process of interpersonal negotiation results in a certain range of beliefs, ideas and ways of doing things which characterize a particular group of people, or even an entire country. It constitutes, in effect, the 'culture' of that country.

Part of the result of this process is that if a person has rather unusual or extreme views on a subject, views which are substantially different to the majority of people, it will not take long before he or she is made aware that their views are indeed very unusual. People may tell them directly, or they may shun their company and avoid discussions with them. In other words, there is considerable social pressure to counteract people proposing unusual views. For example, if I were seriously to propose that I was in contact with an extraterrestrial intelligence which was orbiting the earth in a space ship which looked like a doughnut, I could probably expect, at the very best, to be tolerated as an eccentric.

We, therefore, need to explain why, psychologically, people may be able to accept what most of society regards as completely eccentric ideas. One explanation is that it is not the belief system which is particularly important, but the feeling of social solidarity and companionship which comes from acceptance and membership of a group. In a world which is increasingly individualized, this may be the significant factor. Some people who crave group acceptance may be able to rationalize having an unusual belief system, in order to find that friendship and acceptance. Since they know that they may attract some ridicule in the wider society, this would have the tendency to drive them more and more within the religious movement. Within the security of the latter, they know they are with people who accept them, and who accept their beliefs. The same psychological reassurance may be likely to dissuade them from leaving the group. After a time, it is conceivable that although initially the new member experienced considerable cognitive dissonance with the belief system of the movement, gradually the perceived advantages of membership outweigh the problem of accepting the belief system. Gradually, the cognitive dissonance becomes minimal, and the individual becomes committed to the group.

Another possible explanation for the ability to rationalize beliefs, which are regarded as eccentric in society, is one related to the ego. Some people may wish to appear different and not to hold 'conventional' views. In such a case, even though they may recognize that the world view they are espousing is different from the 'norm', they may still find it attractive to be a member of an unconventional group. For such people it may not be problematic to publicize their views as they may enjoy the sense of being 'different' and holding unusual views.

Finally, it is worth noting the potential for psychological disorientation that exists within the relatively closed society of a new religious movement. When one is a member of a movement in which everyone holds the same views, and where there is a strong psychological commitment to remain within the group, then there is the potential for unusual or even extreme behaviour patterns to emerge. Within such a closed society, the normal social constraints and the slowly developed patterns of acceptable behaviour may be abandoned. New modes of behaviour may develop slowly at first, and then gradually become accepted. Within the parameters of the religious movement, members forget the conventions of the external world, and may start to behave in newer, unconventional ways. As Milne (1987) noted in the context of the Rajneesh movement, it is possible for people to start to behave differently when within the confines of a closed religious system.

In summary then, one could argue that the patterns of behaviour which we develop in society are psychologically fragile. They are subject to constant change and reappraisal, yet within the wider society, the constant checks and balances provided by a complex society prevent, in most cases, people behaving to excess. However, when people are placed within a smaller, closed society, where the same checks and balances are reduced, it is possible for more extreme patterns of behaviour to evolve.

FURTHER READING

Clarke, P. B. (ed.) (1987) *The New Evangelists: Recruitment, Methods and Aims of New Religious Movements*, London: Ethnographica.

Lewis, J. R. (ed.) (1995) *The Gods Have Landed: New Religions from Outer Space*, Albany: State University of New York Press.

Lynch, G. (2007) *The New Spirituality: An Introduction to Progressive Belief in the Twenty-First Century*, London: I.B. Tauris.

Palmer, S. and Hardman, C. (eds) (1999) *Children in New Religions*, New Brunswick: Rutgers University Press.

Richardson, J. T. (ed.) (1978) *Conversion Careers: In and Out of the New Religions*, Beverley Hills: Sage.

CHAPTER 9

GENDER AND DIVERSITY

This chapter examines the role of women in new religious movements, and in particular examines a number of case studies of women who have led religious movements. It also draws attention to the cultural diversity of such women, and poses the question of why their achievements do not appear to have received wider recognition.

LEADERSHIP AND AUTHORITY IN NEW RELIGIOUS MOVEMENTS

The position of the religious teacher in relation to disciples or followers is a very special one. It brings enormous responsibilities to the teacher, and the extent to which those responsibilities are recognized and understood is a measure of the quality of that teacher. The fundamental responsibility of the spiritual teacher is arguably to give of themselves to their followers and not to seek to gain something for themselves. In the case of new religious movements this moral imperative may be all the more significant.

In older religions there is normally a long-established hierarchy which acts to distribute fairly widely, the power and influence within the religion. Even in say the Christian Churches, where there is a single elected leader, the local priest may have considerable influence at a local level with individual church members. However, the idea of spiritual authority is sufficiently distributed for the individual to be able to consult widely when in need of spiritual advice. In the case of new religious movements, however, the locus of spiritual power usually rests with a single person, who may also be the person who started the movement. The result is that members of the movement may all tend to relate to a single spiritual leader – a situation which may bring both advantages and disadvantages. One of the consequences of this is that new religious movements may tend to direct their strategies for recruitment in the direction determined by the leader or founder, with the result that membership of the movement may be over-represented within certain social or occupational categories. For example, the Rajneesh organization, although initially established in India, tended to recruit a significant proportion of Westerners, and apparently a considerable number of relatively affluent and middle-class people, who may have been willing to donate resources to the organization. One might argue then that new religious movements, influenced as many are by a single leader, have a tendency towards developing a monocultural atmosphere with members who share common values and background. This lack of diversity can lead such movements to be more rigid and inflexible in the way they function. It is more difficult for people to criticize the movement internally. If they should do so, it may elicit an antagonistic reaction, and the person may be expelled. This is in contrast generally to established religions where discussion about issues and dissent from the received wisdom is to some extent accepted.

An important concept of contemporary views of society is that of the freedom to think differently to others, and the freedom to articulate those views. Religious teachers, including those within new religious movements, should be able to accept that human beings are not uniform automatons with a single view of the way to attain spiritual understanding. They bring with them their individual concepts of the nature of religion, the spiritual and the Divine, and the ways in which their ultimate vision might be achieved. This is particularly true in relation to women in religion, and notably the role of women within new religious movements. There is little doubt that established religions have been, and are, largely patriarchal in character. Some have tried to justify this on a number of grounds, for example that since a faith has always had men in positions of authority then a priori there must be some divine justification for this. It must somehow be ordained by divine ordinance, or how could it have happened thus? Alternatively, some have argued that religions, in a sense, reflect society, and that as society was extremely male-dominated when many religions were founded, it is hardly surprising that the religion should reflect this within its social structures. Moreover, some would then extend this argument

NEW RELIGIOUS MOVEMENTS: A GUIDE FOR THE PERPLEXED

to suggest the maintenance of the status quo. If religions have been and are male dominated, then why change this when it appears to be functioning acceptably? Without digressing too far to rehearse these arguments here, it does appear as if the majority of these lines of argument take as their starting point the origins of religions at a time in history which was unequivocally patriarchal.

STUDY QUESTION

If religions do reflect the societies in which they evolve and develop, then there would be every reason to suppose that new religious movements might demonstrate a much greater sense of gender equality or even of matriarchal structures. They have after all developed largely during a period of social revolution, and at a time when there are at least some initial signs that society is beginning to reflect gender equality. It would appear, however, that many of the leaders and founders of new religious movements still reflect the male dominance found in traditional religions, although there are instances of women at the head of new movements. Do you think that religions as institutions are particularly resilient to changing attitudes towards gender, or perhaps that society has simply not gone far enough to create genuine gender equality?

WOMEN WHO LEAD NEW RELIGIOUS MOVEMENTS

In the nineteenth century there were significant examples of women who either established or headed new religious movements. Helena Blavatsky (1831–91) was one of the key founders of the Theosophical Society in New York in 1875. This organization was composed of radical religious thinkers, who were committed to the study of different religions around the world, with a particular emphasis upon Indian religious traditions including Buddhism. The Theosophical Society stressed the unity of all humanity, and sought to explore the more esoteric facets of spiritual life. Helena Blavatsky was aided in the latter aim, through her extensive travels and study of different faiths in what were then remote parts of the world. In the mid-nineteenth century she had, for example, travelled to Tibet and studied with Buddhist teachers. She travelled to Sri Lanka in 1880 and formally became a Buddhist. By 1882 she had been instrumental in helping the Society to become a fully international organization and opening a headquarters in Chennai.

One of Helena Blavatsky's followers was another major figure in the history of new religious movements – Annie Besant (1847–1933). She was a person of wide-ranging abilities and intellectual interests. She was one of the great liberal thinkers of her time, being a member of the National Secular Society and also of the Fabian Society. She had strong socialist inclinations and was closely involved in major social causes. In 1888 she protested against the working conditions of the largely female workforce of the Bryant and May match factory in London, where the health of the workers was seriously damaged by the phosphorus used in the production process. She organized a famous strike of the workers, which helped to publicize their situation and resulted in some improvement in the factory conditions. Annie Besant had a strong interest in spiritual matters and joined the Theosophical Society in 1889. She was subsequently asked to attend the Chicago World Fair in 1893, where she spoke about the work and philosophy of the Society. In 1907 she was elected as President of the Theosophical Society. She was a leading advocate for the independence of India from the British, and a close friend and colleague of the leading Indian nationalists and members of the Congress Party in India. A lifelong interest in Hindu culture led to her being instrumental in the founding of Benaras Hindu University, now a leading centre of Sanskrit studies. In addition, she promoted the work and teaching of Krishnamurti, who became one of the leading religious thinkers of his time.

We have already noted earlier in the book, the work of Helen Schucman (1909–81) an academic at Columbia University in New York, who wrote down the results of an 'inner voice' which spoke to her. She took this inner voice to be that of Jesus Christ. The result was A Course in Miracles.

Ellen G. White (1827–1915) was one of the founders of the Seventh-day Adventist Church, now one of the largest religious organizations in the world. Her work was basic to the founding of the Church, whose members believe that she had a profound gift for prophecy and for having visions. She was an extremely prolific writer, whose books, subject to the overall authority of the Bible, are considered an essential element of the theology of the Church. Quite apart from her contribution to directly religious matters, she was also a social reformer, particularly in the area of health care. She was a strong advocate of vegetarianism, not only from a dietary point of view, but also on ethical grounds, as she was very much concerned with the moral aspects of the treatment of animals.

The period from the mid-nineteenth century through to the early decades of the twentieth century was a particularly fruitful time for the establishment of new religions. This was particularly so in the United States in connection with religions related to Christianity. Moreover, a number of these new religions were established by women. Given the male dominance of society generally at this period, it is not easy to explain the evident acceptance of women starting new religious movements. Nonetheless, it is quite clear that some extremely talented and charismatic women were able to found major new religious initiatives and to attract a wide range of followers.

Mary Baker Eddy (1821–1910) was the founder of the Christian Science movement. She also founded the celebrated journal *The Christian Science Monitor*. Born in New Hampshire, she appears to have been from an early age, a very independent thinker, and not necessarily accepting of her parents' religious views as Congregationalists. She became particularly interested in the centrality of healing as an element in Christianity, and there is some evidence of her capacity as a spiritual healer. She certainly believed in her capacity to use her Christian beliefs to help her heal people. She asserted that by concentrating on the spirit of God, she could bring to bear that spirituality in healing others. Many of the more modern treatments for illness were rejected by Eddy on the grounds that Jesus did not employ such methods, and that she therefore preferred to employ spiritual healing methods. To Eddy all of the evidence seemed to point to the potential efficacy of spiritual healing, and that this approach was in a sense 'scientific'. She believed that she had developed a precise approach to spiritual healing, and that she was capable of helping her followers to understand and use such techniques. Her healing approach was outlined in her 1875 book *Science and Health with Key to the Scriptures* which became an important text of Christian Science. The book was studied by her followers who also wanted to be involved in spiritual healing. Her teachings as part of the Christian Science movement were disseminated across the United States by her followers, and the publications she founded also helped in this. Apart from the *Christian Science Monitor*, she also established the *Christian Science Journal* and the *Christian Science Sentinel*.

Among her many achievements, Mary Baker Eddy recognized the potential of the printed media in gaining followers, spreading her ideas and generally gaining support for her developing Church. This was also true of Aimee Semple McPherson (1890–1944) the founder of the Foursquare Church, who employed every facet of the then-available media to publicize her teachings and Church. A Canadian by birth, McPherson became involved in the work of the Salvation Army because of the interest of her parents. In 1908 she became a member of the Pentecostal Church, although subsequently continued her work with the Salvation Army, providing food and clothing to those in need. By the age of 23, Aimee McPherson started to hold religious meetings and to preach her ideas of Christianity. She was clearly a charismatic preacher and managed to attract considerable attendance at her meetings. She held spiritual meetings in a number of different states including California. Like Mary Baker Eddy, she was also interested in the healing aspects of her religious calling, and developed something of a reputation as a healer. An equal enthusiasm for McPherson was her opposition to the teaching of evolution in schools. She felt very strongly that this was antithetical to her religious beliefs, and did her best to campaign against the place of evolution in the curriculum. Between 1917 and 1918 McPherson started to do a considerable amount of writing, publishing articles particularly on the position of women in society and especially within religious organizations. She was able, in this way, to attract considerable numbers of female members to the Foursquare Gospel Church. In some ways, McPherson could be described as a religious traditionalist, but she managed in the public arena, particularly through her involvement with the media, to portray herself as a very contemporary figure, and this no doubt helped her in attracting new members to her Church. She was somewhat critical of the practice of churches organizing many social events as an extension of the religious activities of a church. She felt that spiritual and religious activities were the key responsibility of a church, rather than being a focus for community entertainment of any kind. The organization she founded gradually became better and better known, and assumed the full name of the International Church of the Foursquare Gospel.

Within her movement Aimee McPherson stressed a number of key religious beliefs and principles. Central to these was a profound belief in the positive influence of Jesus Christ on the lives of individual people. She believed deeply in the reality of the second-coming of Jesus Christ to earth, and in the capacity of Jesus, mediated through human beings on earth, to heal people. The Foursquare Gospel Church advocated the sacrament of baptism, and stressed that sincere believers and members of the Church would be saved from their sins and find the Kingdom of God through the grace of Jesus.

McPherson became famous for her preaching, and in particular for the almost theatrical presentations which accompanied her church services. In 1924 the Foursquare Church purchased a radio station for broadcasting religious services and programmes. This could be argued to be a precursor to the later widespread use of the media for religious purposes and in particular the practice of television evangelism. She continued to argue strongly against the teaching of evolution in schools, suggesting that the concept of social Darwinism was fundamentally unethical. McPherson never ceased to be involved in charitable work for people who were disadvantaged, and particularly during the economic depression of the 1930s, she arranged for the distribution of food and clothing to those in need. Finally, Aimee McPherson felt strongly about racial equality, and within the context of her Church, did her best to further opportunities for the African American and Spanish-speaking communities.

There has always tended to be a strong involvement of African Americans in Christian Church movements, particularly in the United States, and women have often played major roles in these developments. Notable in this context was Ida B. Robinson (1891–1946), an African American woman who founded the Mount Sinai Holy Church of America. One of her key contributions was that she wanted to encourage women to become preachers, and within her Church she always tried to invite women to speak to the congregation. As a young woman she lived in Philadelphia, and became a member of the United Holy Church of America. Later she became ordained within this Church. When she was 33 years of age, she started to feel that God was revealing his ultimate purpose for her. She felt that God was impelling her towards the establishment of a new Church – one in which women would have a very significant role. She wanted women to be ordained and to have major roles within her Church. In 1924 she obtained official permission to establish a new Church which was to be called The Mount Sinai

Holy Church of America, Incorporated. True to her beliefs in full opportunities for women, Ida Robinson ensured that a majority of the management roles of the new Church were held by women. The Church expanded rapidly, and by the time of her death in 1946, there were almost 100 individual churches within the overall denomination.

There are also examples of new religious movements founded in other parts of the world by women. Tenrikyo, a religious movement of Japanese origin, is now a genuinely world religion, with something in the region of two million members. It was founded by Nakayama Miki (1798–1887). Miki was born into a Buddhist family, but in middle age she started to feel that she was receiving communications from God, who wanted her to be the 'shrine of God'. God is known by members of Tenrikyo as 'God the Parent'.

Miki wrote down many of the communications which she received from God the Parent, and told her followers that she had the power to heal and the power of prophecy. She made great efforts to provide food and other material assistance to the poor and disadvantaged. To some extent she alienated the Buddhist hierarchy of the country, although on the other hand, it appears as if Miki synthesized a variety of religious ideas from both Buddhism and Shinto into her new religious movement.

Members of Tenrikyo believe that they are autonomous human beings who can determine their own course of action in life, but that their bodies are created by God, and given to them by God, to be returned when they die. One can see a potential connection here with the Buddhist doctrine of impermanence. Tenrikyo places great emphasis in its teachings on providing assistance to those in need. Another similarity with Buddhist teaching is that members of Tenrikyo do not regard bad or immoral deeds as something for which the individual human being must atone. Rather they are seen as the result of an inappropriate understanding of the world, which can be corrected by trying hard to see the world more clearly. In a similar way, followers of Tenrikyo have a very philosophical attitude to the inevitable problems of life. They try to look at such problems in a balanced and objective manner, and try not to become too obsessed with them. One is reminded again of the calm rationalism of Buddhism. Tenrikyo is not a religious movement which demands close conformity to a strict ideology or set of teachings. It accepts that to a certain extent human beings will want to find their own way to a spiritual goal, and indeed encourages that sense of autonomy. Throughout its history, Tenrikyo has interacted considerably with both Buddhist and Shinto teaching, although followers argue consistently that the particular spiritual vision of Nakayama Miki was a distinctive one.

A completely different religious tradition is provided by the new religious movement of Kemetic Orthodoxy. This is a movement devoted to the religious philosophy and deities of ancient Egypt, and was established by Tamara Siuda in the late 1980s. Siuda studied Egyptology at university, and felt that she had been inspired to disseminate belief in the deities of ancient Egypt. Central beliefs of the movement include a respect for ma'at, which is held to be the spiritual influence which permeates the universe, and which maintains a sense of equilibrium throughout the world. Although the cultures are very different, and there is no suggestion that one has influenced the other, one is reminded here of the concept of the Tao in Chinese thought. Another key belief is in the ultimate God of the Kemetic tradition called Netjer. Kemetic Orthodoxy could be described as an attempted reconstruction of the religious life of ancient Egypt, although Siuda also introduces her own interpretations, a practice not uncommon where a spiritual tradition is reconstructed from incomplete historical records. Siuda is respected by members of this new religious movement, as a legitimate spiritual teacher who can act as an intermediary between the deities and followers of Kemetic Orthodoxy. There is a consistent attempt to reflect, in contemporary practice, the religious customs and social patterns of ancient Egypt.

India has always tended to be a country within which the contribution of women to religious life has been widely acknowledged and encouraged. The feminine within religious life is recognized in the Hindu faith, with for example, the holy river Ganges, being referred to as Mata Ganga, or Mother Ganges. Sahaja Yoga is a new religious movement founded by Nirmala Srivastava, often referred to as Shri Mataji Nirmala Devi. She was born in 1923 in Chindawara, India. Her parents were colleagues of Mahatma Gandhi in the fight for Indian independence, and during the period of the Second World War, Nirmala herself worked for the Congress Party, being at one stage imprisoned by the British authorities. A lifelong interest in the Hindu spiritual tradition lead her in 1970 to establish the Sahaja Yoga movement, dedicated to enabling people to experience the awakening of the kundalini or potential spiritual energy which is present in all of us. She developed and taught systems of meditation which would enable this to happen. Nirmala has consistently encouraged her followers to investigate and test the meditational strategies which she has advocated, rather than simply accepting them because they have been taught by her. She has also been a firm critic of Indian gurus and teachers who have founded new religious movements, and who appear to offer their teaching in exchange for large financial contributions. She apparently attended a Rajneesh commune at one time, and was very critical of some of the practices she found there. The self-realization, which results from the awakening of the kundalini energy, is said to be accompanied by feelings of contentment, peace, equanimity and a sense of being in harmony with the world. The practice of sahaja meditation is also claimed by the movement to have considerable health benefits including the lowering of states of hypertension and decreasing stress levels. The movement has founded a number of schools and community centres. Nirmala has visited many of the major countries of the world, giving lectures and passing on the principles of sahaja yoga. She has received honours of various kinds in a number of countries, and continues to adhere to her practice of not charging fees for tuition in Sahaja Yoga.

Finally in this review of the role of women in establishing new religious movements, it is important not to forget an Englishwoman, Ann Lee, who was one of the founders, and then the leader of the Shaker movement. We are now very familiar with Shaker design, and particularly with regard to the simple, solid furniture, for which the Shakers are famous. What is less well-known perhaps, and less celebrated, is the revolutionary approach of gender equality which they practised under Ann Lee's leadership.

The Shakers or United Society of Believers in Christ's Second Appearing began as a very small community in about 1747 in England, and Ann Lee became their acknowledged leader round about 1760. Ann Lee had been born in Manchester in 1736 and died in New York State in 1784. She and her followers met considerable persecution and opposition in England, and she migrated to the United States in 1774, with a small group of followers. Here she established a number of small Shaker communities, which lived a quiet, diligent life according to the principles which Ann Lee had established.

The movement was originally known as the Shakers or Shaking Quakers because of the dancing and shaking which often accompanied their acts of worship. Celibacy and abstaining from marriage was a major tenet of the movement. Ann Lee argued that this was a better way to lead a spiritual and religious life. Men and women within the Shaker communities tended to lead separate lives, meeting only under relatively controlled circumstances. An important principle of Shaker religious life was that women were considered able to provide spiritual guidance and leadership just as much as men. The administrative leadership of communities was shared equally between men and women. Interestingly, from a theological viewpoint, there was the concept that God incorporated both genders simultaneously – a rather radical concept for the time, and perhaps even now. The work of a Shaker community was largely shared between men and women with both genders participating in the physical work necessary to support the community. There was no sense in which the work of women was perceived as of lesser importance to that of the men. The work and lifestyle of Shaker communities became very famous. They were run very efficiently, with their farms being a model of cleanliness and efficient production. They espoused virtues of modesty, diligence, care and humility in all they did. The Shaker way of life gradually declined throughout the twentieth century, largely because of the philosophy of not supporting marriage, and therefore the absence of children to sustain the way of life. The Shaker communities have now practically disappeared, but the way of life has remained an inspiration for many, and their ideas sustained by the nature of the objects they created, as a reflection of a particular spiritual existence.

This review of the role of women in founding new religious movements demonstrates the relatively widespread involvement of women, not only in the United Kingdom and United States, but in other countries and cultures. There appears to be evidence that not only have women been involved in the founding of new movements, but that men have been inspired by their leadership, and became their followers. Perhaps what is required is that the involvement of women in new religious movements should be more widely disseminated, and that this may then influence their increased involvement within the power and authority structures of longer-established religions.

FURTHER READING

Eller, C. (1993) *Living in the Lap of the Goddess: The Feminist Spirituality Movement in America*, New York: Crossroad.

Hutton, R. (1999) *Triumph of the Moon: A History of Modern Pagan Witchcraft*, Oxford: Oxford University Press.

Palmer, S. J. (1994) *Moon Sisters, Krishna Mothers, Rajneesh Lovers: Women's Roles in New Religions*, Syracuse: Syracuse University Press.

Puttick, E. (1997) *Women in New Religions: In Search of Community, Sexuality, and Spiritual Power*, New York: St Martins Press.

Sharma, A. (ed.) (1994) *Today's Woman in World Religions*, Albany: State University of New York Press.

CHAPTER 10

POWER AND AUTHORITY

This chapter examines the nature of authority in new religious movements and the various mechanisms by which it operates. It explores the way in which values are reinforced, and also examines the approaches of charismatic leaders in the exercise of power. There is also an analysis of the development of dependency in new members.

THE INFLUENCE OF GROUP NORMS

One of the major areas of contention in the discussions of new religious movements is that of the distribution of power and authority within them. The received wisdom and perhaps the commonest analysis tends to be a variant of the idea that the movement's leader exercises considerable control over the members. This authority is commonly described as charismatic, and there are often suggestions that the autonomy of individual members is restricted such that they appear to have limited control over their own actions and decisions. There are often suggestions that individuals, and particularly new members, allow themselves to be subservient to the norms of the group, even when those norms are at odds with accepted patterns of behaviour in external society. Further, it is sometimes alleged that groups encourage, or indeed attempt to impose, access to external society. This may mean that individual members are discouraged from contacting their families or their former friends. In more extreme cases, they may be explicitly required not to make such contacts. This is no doubt a stereotypical picture of the power relations within a new religious movement, but it provides a starting point for an analysis of such power and authority.

One of the functions of most religions whether large or small, new or long-established, is that they try to provide some guidance to human beings on the way in which they should lead their lives. One way in which they try to do this is through the mechanism of moral prescription. In the case of long-established religions such ethical precepts are often written down, codified and carry the imprimatur of scriptural authority. New religious movements, however, are usually much smaller in terms of numbers of adherents, at least in their early stages of development, and with regard to moral codes may rely much more on interpersonal guidance from senior members of the movement or from the teacher or founder. As a new religious movement grows, systems of ways of behaving, of speaking in meeting, or social discourse, and of communication develop. When new members join the movement they are socialized into these systems, and often fairly quickly become attuned to the idea of the objective validity of these norms. The newcomer will often try very hard to adhere to these norms and values, at least partly in order to be accepted within the group.

However, apart from the general membership and in particular the senior members, the other principal source of moral guidance is the teacher, guru or founder of the movement. This individual will have probably been central in developing these norms, and will continue to be influential in their application. It is argued by some, such as Bird (1979) that compared with the long-established religions, members of new religious movements tend to intervene in moral situations, and to exercise their sense of moral autonomy, to a much lesser extent. According to Bird, this 'occurs in all types of movements, and it constitutes for participants one of the appealing aspects of these new religions' (1979, p. 335). There may be a sense here, that in a smaller group, it is much easier for someone to submit themselves to the collective value system, and to abrogate to a certain degree, their sense of moral responsibility. The act of exercising our moral autonomy and sense of responsibility is not always an easy thing to do. It can sometimes set us in conflict with our peers, and in extreme cases, we can find ourselves on our own, defending what may seem to be an unpopular or minority viewpoint. The newcomer to a relatively small religious movement is probably not going to wish to do this. It seems much more likely that they will want to conform to group norms and consolidate their membership of the movement. In addition, small groups tend to be rather more uniform in their norms and opinions than larger groups. The latter may be sufficiently complex in structure, to enable them to harbour a range of opinions and values. Authority may be much more dispersed in such a group, and hence it is less likely that a minority viewpoint will be alienating to any great degree. This is possibly the case in large, long-established religions.

As argued above, it is not always an attractive proposition to challenge group values. To do so first demands that we do a considerable amount of thinking in order to establish and analyse our position on an issue, and secondly we have to be assertive in arguing for that position, often in the face of considerable opposition. It is certainly easier, at least in the short term, and certainly the line of least resistance, to simply accept the ethical norms of the group, and not to try to assert our own views. It would appear that in some cases this is what happens within new religious movements. In the case of a benign and morally responsible religious group, the consequences may be minimal. However, in the case of a group which has evolved extreme or amoral values, the consequences can be that members do not challenge behaviour which in the external society would be viewed as completely unacceptable or even criminal. Ultimately, one can argue that as rational human beings we must all be willing to exercise our moral autonomy, and if necessary to assert the validity of our moral judgements, however unpopular that may make us.

SOME ASPECTS OF CHARISMA

One of the most important elements in encouraging or discouraging moral independence is the leader or teacher of a new religious movement. One of the most frequently reported qualities associated with a teacher in a new religious movement is that of 'charisma'. A newcomer may be attracted to a movement initially for a variety of reasons, often with the initial contact being with ordinary members. However, it is often the leader who ultimately cements that commitment to the movement and reinforces a long-term membership and association. Members of new religious movements often assert that their teacher or guru possesses a range of qualities which they find inspirational and motivating. They may suggest that their guru inspires in them such intense feelings of love and affection that they feel all their anxieties are lifted from them, and they feel completely at peace in the presence of their teacher. In addition, they may ascribe to their teacher healing abilities or the capacity to generate mystical or spiritual experiences. Some people may also suggest that their teacher generates a feeling of unity within them; that they feel united with both their guru and also with the universe as a whole. No longer do they feel to be an isolated human being, addressing the world in solitude, but there is a feeling that they are part, not only of the sum total of humanity, but also that they are somehow part of the spiritual force of the universe.

Some or all of these emotions, feelings and qualities are part of what may commonly be referred to as charisma. Members in many new religious movements have attributed this quality to the leader of their religion, without necessarily analysing its nature. An interesting philosophical question concerning charisma is whether it can exist in an individual, if no one is present to perceive it. Would it make logical sense to describe someone as charismatic, if for the sake of argument, they lived the life of a hermit, and never met anyone? How in that case, one may ask, could we possibly know that they were charismatic? Hence, is not charisma a quality which must be perceived and appreciated, in order that its existence might be confirmed? We might imagine, for example, a guru surrounded by disciples. No matter how much the guru wished to be seen as charismatic, this could only be confirmed and validated if the disciples actually agreed that the guru was in fact demonstrating charisma. In other words, charisma is a quality which is defined in terms of the interaction between people. It is not a quality which inheres in someone simply by virtue of its own objective existence. In fact, one might argue that when members of a new religious movement recognize charismatic qualities in their leader, they are reinforcing and enhancing those very qualities. DuPertuis (1986, p. 113) suggests that 'People, whether or not they are fully conscious of so doing, thus help to create the objects of their devotion.'

Of all the leaders of new religious movements, one of the archetypal charismatic leaders was no doubt Rajneesh. As Palmer (1988, p. 122) suggests, 'His charismatic authority is based on his claim to be the "Enlightened One" who returns throughout the millennia to awaken spiritually an elite group of seekers.' Now this claim to authority can never be fully validated or authenticated in an objective sense. It can, however, be 'believed'. It can, to his followers, be an entirely acceptable and plausible assertion. I will not say 'reasonable' claim, since its validation is outside the scope of objective rationality. Nevertheless, it can be entirely believable. However, there is nothing intrinsic about the claim that Rajneesh returns to this earth, on occasions often many years apart to enlighten people, which might make us believe him. We only believe him if we wish to believe him. Thus he acquires his charismatic authority, only if his followers wish to attribute this quality to him.

DEPENDENCY UPON THE LEADER AND ORGANIZATION

It can be assumed that all leaders, whether of religious or other organizations, do on some occasions feel vulnerable and wonder about their capacity to hold on to their power and position. Johnson (1979) argues that this is true of charismatic religious leaders, and in terms of consolidating their authority suggests that 'one strategy is to make the members as dependent as possible upon the leader . . .' (p. 316). Now there are various forms of dependency and in order for the members of a new religious movement to be dependent on their leader or teacher, they have to, either consciously or unconsciously, collaborate in establishing such a relationship. A person who is by nature independent in character will not succumb to a relationship which is fundamentally dependent. They will value their autonomy, and will simply not acquiesce to such a relationship.

In the case, however, of some members of new religious movements, there may be a variety of factors which contribute to a culture of dependency. They may be individuals who are psychologically vulnerable or are perhaps passing through a period in their lives when they feel rather vulnerable. This may well be the case with young people in their late teens and twenties, which perhaps explains why some movements particularly aim their recruitment at such age groups. It is also often the case that young people are going through a phase when they reject the advice of their families and parents and want to demonstrate that they are able to establish themselves in the world independently. Joining a new religious movement, with the promise of regular meals and accommodation, may thus be very attractive. Young people may not necessarily realize that they are potentially or actually placing themselves in a position of dependency. If the organization asks them to refrain from contacting their parents, this may not seem particularly problematic, since they may already be at least partially alienated from their family.

STUDY QUESTION

People may become dependent upon a religious movement and upon the principal teacher, because they are passing through a phase in life, when they seek some sense of meaning or self-actualization in their lives. They may be experiencing difficulties with their career, or with their marriage, or in some other way, and may feel the need for an alternative way in which they can validate their lives. They may feel such a sense of well-being when they find a new religious movement which accepts and welcomes them, and provides them with a feeling of unconditional support, that they become extremely dependent upon it. They may submit themselves so entirely, that they simply do not realize the extent to which they have become dependent upon the movement and the leader. How far can dependency go before it becomes undesirable? What are acceptable limits of such dependency?

Some may also become dependent upon a new religious movement by virtue of physical need. The unemployed, homeless, or those who are for some reason finding it very hard to survive in society may be attracted to a movement simply because they are looked after and fed. The religious belief system may initially be a fairly peripheral issue for them, in comparison with the need for food and shelter, but gradually they may be drawn in to the behavioural norms of the group. They may also develop a considerable sense of indebtedness to the teacher for providing them with a home. All in all, this will again represent a situation of dependency, the outcome of which may be a little uncertain.

The leader of a group may strengthen his or her influence over the members by encouraging a close sense of belonging within the movement. In a situation where there is a very close feeling of social cohesion, where the bonds between the individual members are very strong, a situation may be reached where the individual members only wish to relate to other members. In such a case, it is easier for a leader to control and even manipulate the members, since they may come to act almost as a single entity.

There are a variety of strategies or circumstances which may bring about a situation such as this. The members, upon joining the movement, may all be given the same scripture to read and discuss, the same prayers to learn or the same meditational techniques to practice. The result may be that they increasingly relate only to other members of the group, and not to people outside the movement. It may not be that there is any deliberate attempt to isolate the movement from the outside world, but the end result is that members simply feel more at ease, and interact better with the members of the movement. Bainbridge and Stark (1979, p. 293) term such a situation, a 'social implosion'. This type of development is likely to increase the power and authority of the leader of the movement.

New religious movements need to finance their activities in just the same way as any other organization. They usually need to finance property and its upkeep, marketing and printing costs, and ongoing revenue items like food and electricity. Money is typically raised by a variety of means including the sale of publications, religious artefacts and products such as incense and statues, fees charged for study courses or for residence, and membership charges and donations. Larger movements may also have considerable investments which generate interest and profits.

In comparison with long-established religions, denominations and churches which may have considerable historical investments in property and land, new religious movements are not generally able to rely upon income from such sources. In older religions it may not be as necessary to receive large amounts of money or other contributions from members, as income is available from other sources. However, in the case of new movements, it is important for the leader to utilize all the available resources of members. The economic contribution, according to Bird and Westley (1985, p. 169) often consists of 'a highly involved inner core of adepts and a large and transient body of affiliates and clients'. The central body of very committed members may not only contribute considerable amounts of personal money to the organization, but may also work very hard in all kinds of ways to enhance the economic effectiveness of the movement. In short, they may help in working on all kinds of projects associated with the movement, whether that be by carring out physical, manual work, or by teaching or running courses. In some cases, they may continue to work in salaried jobs outside the organization, while contributing a large part of that income to the organization. Clearly, the more a leader can encourage that kind of commitment, the more it benefits the religious movement, and indeed probably strengthens his or her position.

However, the status of new religious movements in society, and with it the way in which movement leaders are perceived, has from time to time come under attack from opponents of such movements. Some countries are perhaps, by virtue of the nature of their societal structures, more open to the idea of new religious movements than others. In France, where the Roman Catholic Church still tends to exert considerable influence, and where it also remains an agent of social cohesion, there is considerable scepticism concerning new religious movements. Beckford (1981, p. 257) argues that the movement of the The Three Holy Hearts, which was active in the 1970s, has done more than any other cult to generate a negative feeling in France towards such organizations. Undoubtedly, the extreme behaviour within some movements around the world has contributed towards the antipathy felt by many people towards new religious movements. This continues to make it difficult for the leaders of movements to attain social legitimacy, and must to some extent make it more difficult to recruit new members and for the leader to exercise influence and authority.

New religious movements and their leaders tend also to find themselves alienated from the greater society, depending upon the extent to which the movement appears to wish to change society. The more substantial the desired or potential change, then the more society is likely to react against the leader. Shupe and Bromley (1979, p. 326) make this argument with regard to the Unification Church and its non-acceptance of traditional Christian teaching.

Very often the leaders of new religious movement may appear to apply different standards to themselves, as opposed to those they define for the members. Relatively rarely do we find a new religious movement where the assets and wealth of the organization are not under the centralized control of the leadership. In some cases that control amounts to access to very considerable amounts of money. The leaders of some new religious movements do not appear to recognize any moral imperative to treat members as equal to themselves. As they have founded the movement, it is as if they feel they have the legitimacy to determine the group norms and to impose those, irrespective of fairness or a sense of democratic decision-making.

Upal (2005a) used the term 'information entrepreneurs' (p. 229) to describe the leaders of new religious movements. He likened them in many ways to those influential individuals in many walks of life including academia, the arts, politics, the media or finance, for example, who develop their influence by disseminating ideas which attract the attention of people. The interesting element which distinguishes the entrepreneurs who found religious movements is that they link a spiritual aspect to the ideas which they pass on. Indeed he argues that they in effect place themselves in a position between the divine and the members of his organization. They are thus in a very influential position to interpret for people, the way they should act and respond to the world. The leader can always argue that he or she has been privy to the word of the divine, and in the context of that it becomes less easy for members to challenge the leader's assertions.

Upal argues that all information entrepreneurs seek rewards for their role and their actions, and that this applies just as much to religious information entrepreneurs as to those in other areas of activity. While entrepreneurs in some spheres of activity may be motivated primarily by monetary rewards, this may or may not apply to religious entrepreneurs. The latter may often be largely motivated by the acquisition of power and the desire to exercise influence and control over members of their organization.

In a separate article Upal (2005b) suggests that the founders and leaders of new religious movements have 'the additional pleasure of serving God, who they believe is guiding them' (para 2.1). If a person comes to believe unshakably that God is fulfilling his or her message through them, then this can initiate a very powerful sense of their own self-importance. It may give them the conviction that it is their destiny to found a religious movement and to recruit members to that movement. In addition, it may provide them with a form of psychological justification for the way they structure the movement, the manner in which they behave to the members and the strategies they employ to find new recruits. Thus, this type of self-induced world view may from a psychological point of view, act not only as a motivator, but also as an instrument to distort the leader's view of reality.

One of the most contentious of the policies of some movement leaders has been the apparently deliberate diminution in the influence of the family within new religions. Where parents with younger children join a movement, this has sometimes taken the form of discouraging parental authority over the children. The latter are often encouraged to loosen their association with their natural parents and to view themselves as a collective family of the movement. The religious movement gradually assumes responsibility for the children, with the parents being released to carry out work for the organization. The parents then have a generalized responsibility for the children. The result of this is that gradually some of the inter-familial bonds may weaken, and within such an amorphous structure, there is the possibility that the influence of the leader will be enhanced. Whitsett and Kent (2003) argue that leaders may sometimes reduce considerably the psychological links within families. The leader of the movement may then become a sort of figurehead parent for the whole organization, and for all the children and young people within it. In the most benign of circumstances, this may not have any particularly serious consequences, although the results of such communal responsibility for children may not have been adequately researched or documented. However, in the most extreme and controlling of situations, such as that created by David Koresh mentioned earlier, the result may be a regime which involves exploitation and abuse. Therefore, particularly where children, through their parents, live within a communal religious context, it seems desirable that the sanctity of the family unit is maintained, and secondly that adults and parents within the movement are particularly sensitive and watchful concerning any possible incursions into their autonomy and natural responsibility for their children.

FURTHER READING

Bromley, D. G. and Melton, J. G. (eds) (2002) *Cults, Religion and Violence*, Cambridge: Cambridge University Press.

Galanter, M. (1989) *Cults: Faith, Healing, and Coercion*, New York: Oxford University Press.

Jenkins, P. (2000) *Mystics and Messiahs: Cults and New Religions in American History*, Oxford: Oxford University Press.

Wessinger, C. (2000) *How the Millennium Comes Violently: From Jonestown to Heaven's Gate*, New York: Seven Bridges.

Zablocki, B. and Robbins, T. (eds) (2001) *Misunderstanding Cults: Searching for Objectivity in a Controversial Field*, Toronto: University of Toronto Press.

CHAPTER 11

POSTMODERNISM AND THE DEVELOPMENT OF NEW RELIGIOUS MOVEMENTS

The chapter analyses the historical development of the postmodern era and of the characteristics of society during this period. It examines theoretical perspectives on the nature of postmodern society, and relates these to changes in religion, and in particular to the tendencies towards eclecticism in religion, and the development of new religious movements.

CHANGES IN THE NATURE OF SOCIETY

As we have seen, there is considerable evidence of the development of new religious ideas and movements during the nineteenth and early twentieth centuries. However, it was often the case that the new developments extended or adapted established religions such as Christianity. The large-scale expansion of different, unusual or reconstructed religions only really took place after the Second World War and in particular from the decade of the 1960s onwards. This has been a very interesting development, and merits an attempt at explaining it in terms of broader transitions in society. One could simply argue that the 1960s was a period of enhanced liberalism in terms of social attitudes, and that this encouraged the proliferation of new minority faiths. However, this appears to be potentially a rather simplistic and superficial explanation, and the issue really deserves an examination of the more profound changes in society during the past 50 years or so, which could have had an effect on the creation of new religious movements.

Prior to the Second World War, the countries which formed the major aggregations of political power in the world subscribed to specific political, ideological and economic systems. A Marxist-Leninist ideology combined with a centralized economy characterized the then Soviet Union, compared with a participative democracy in the West adopting a mixed economic system of a free market with some elements of directive social control. By and large, the world was typified by sweeping ideological systems, which held sway over the lives of many millions of people and provided the dominant world views for many countries. Not only the political and economic systems, but also legal, judicial, health and most notable education systems were influenced by, if not subject to, these dominant world views.

But by the 1960s the world was showing signs of major changes, indeed revolution. The war in Vietnam was causing particularly young people to question the efficacy and morality of American foreign policy, while racial tensions in the United States were a continual source of social conflict. The 1968 student riots in Paris demonstrated that there were undercurrents of social dissatisfaction which were subverting society. Meanwhile the inefficiencies of the Soviet economic system presaged the gradual collapse of that political system and the disintegration and subsequent fragmentation of the Soviet Union. It was thus a period during which the old certainties were being challenged and demonstrated themselves inadequate in being able to absorb the challenges and conflicts of a changing world. It was a gradual worldwide process which involved a transition from the aggregation, cohesion and synthesis of ideas towards the dissipation and fragmentation of ideas. The previously dominant ideologies started to collapse, resulting in a great diversification of ideas and systems.

STUDY QUESTION

Michel Foucault, a leading French intellectual who was active in the social changes of the late 1960s, highlighted the transition from centralized power typified by the Church and monarchical authority in the medieval period to the increasingly dispersed power of the late modern and postmodern periods. He commented on the change from sweeping ideological systems to more individualized perspectives on the world. As you look around the world, do you think authority, and particularly religious authority, is becoming more de-centralized?

There were also demands for far more equality in society, in terms of gender, race and sexual orientation. Initial legislation in the areas of race and gender in the late 1960s anticipated an increasing momentum for equality in pay for men and women, and in other areas of society such as for the recognition of same-gender marriage. The general trend was towards a much more plural society. It was as if there was an increasingly common accord that there was not just one way of organizing human society, but there were many different ways, and indeed there was an increasing realization that it was in principle possible, for diversity to coexist, and for diversity, not uniformity, to form the basis of a balanced and fair society.

We were indeed moving from a modern society to a postmodern society. One of the key features of that change was to challenge the existence of universally agreed, non-contestable truths. Since the Enlightenment there had been a belief in rationality and science as the keys to progress, and yet in a postmodern world, it started to become apparent that science and technology were not necessarily panaceas for society. There was a growing acceptance that the by-products of energy consumption were having an adverse effect on the planet. The received wisdom that unrestricted technological advance was a priori a good thing began to be challenged.

As we moved into a postmodern world, the notion of universal, objectively verifiable truth was increasingly challenged, in all spheres of life. This was also true of the established religions, where people were less and less inclined to permit a hierarchical theocracy to interpret the world for them, and to delineate the way in which their lives should be lead. Rather truth was increasingly seen as relative rather than absolute. Certainties were replaced with uncertainties, and people began learning to live with plurality and diversity. Knowledge was increasingly perceived as a social construction (Berger and Luckmann, 1967). In other words, knowledge was not seen as emerging from authority structures in society, or from the accepted truths of ancient cultures, but was seen as evolving from interpersonal discussion and debate. Knowledge was seen as being continually created through the interactions of people. One person proposed an idea; another challenged it, and out of this emerged a synthesis. Such a dialectical process was seen as central to knowledge creation.

THE CHALLENGE TO THE 'META-NARRATIVE'

In the postmodern world there developed a feeling that what the French philosopher, Jean-Francois Lyotard (1986, p. 34) referred to as 'meta-narratives' were inadequate to represent the increasing complexity of the world and of human reflection on it. A meta-narrative is seen as any sweeping belief-system, which by virtue of its scope and scale, seeks to interpret the world within the parameters of a grand perspective. Political ideologies such as Marxism or free-market economics would be examples of meta-narratives. In addition, the assertion that science and technology can be used to endlessly improve the world is a meta-narrative. What is more, religions themselves are meta-narratives. Each religion attempts to provide a cohesive, integrated system of thought, which may be used, according to its advocates, to support all aspects of an individual's existence. It is not to say that there is not some truth and value in all meta-narratives, but rather that in postmodernity, there is an increasing trend towards considering them inadequate to provide a complete explanation of the human condition. It is thus that we begin to see a potential explanation for the rise of new religious movements. In a world in which people are no longer satisfied with unidimensional explanation, it becomes more and more attractive to either adapt an established religion to reflect one's own particular views, or indeed to establish a completely new religious system.

However, the replacement of grand theory by an almost infinite variety of individual preferences and ideas can lead to uncertainty, and this can be potentially disconcerting. Arlandson (2007) writes that 'to move from the modern to the postmodern is to embrace skepticism about what our culture stands for and strives for'. Now there is nothing wrong with challenging ideas and existing theories. In fact this is the way in which the advances of the Enlightenment were made. However, within postmodernity, the challenge for individual people is how to develop a credible philosophy of life, in an environment of an almost infinite number of competing ideas. Within such a society there are no longer any certainties. Everyone is, in a sense, required to develop their own world view and value system. Not everyone, however, may either be inclined to do this, or feel that they are able to do it.

One of the arguments against meta-narratives in modernity is that they tended to support the existing hierarchical power structures of society. Indeed, in some cases the meta-narrative actually was the power structure, as in the case of Marxism-Leninism. However, to replace such grand-narratives with a multiplicity of smaller narratives is not necessarily a happy alternative. It can lead, in the case of new religious movements, to a wide range of small organizations, each with its own power system of authority and control. This may not necessarily be undesirable, if the system is broadly democratic and participative, but this may not be so. We have seen examples of new religious movements, such as the Branch Davidians, where power was very centralized, and where there was apparently no effective system of balance or control to limit the power of the movement's leader.

One argument in favour of the philosophy of postmodernism is that it reflects naturally occurring features of the universe and of the social world in which we live. The universe may be capable of being described and interpreted in terms of certain physical laws and, depending upon one's point of view, may be divinely ordained and inspired. However, it appears also to be subject to many apparently random events which seem to defy prediction. The result is that many view the universe as being essentially in a state of chaos. Some would argue, therefore, that grand-narratives are almost, by their very nature, contrary to the normal state of the universe and human society. Such an argument would propose that diversity and non-conformity are in fact more 'normal' than uniformity. Transferring this idea to the study of new religious movements, one might propose that it is perfectly reasonable to have a situation where individual human beings develop their own particular views on religious and spiritual issues. Some might argue that it runs contrary to the idea of human nature to suppose that human beings might think so uniformly that they could subscribe to the same religious doctrine. However, if it is open for every single individual to, in principle, create their own religion, we might feel we are left with a very uncertain world. In such a world, there would be no consistency of belief, and no common agreement about ethical values.

STUDY QUESTION

Jean-Paul Sartre, the existentialist writer and philosopher, argued that each individual was free to mould their life as they saw fit. However, that freedom also brought with it a certain anxiety, as we realize the enormity of our personal responsibility. If we create our own belief system, then we must also accept the possible consequences. What do you think of this dilemma?

Certainly, ethical values do not need necessarily to derive from religion, but in reality many have evolved from religious principles. The three monotheistic religions of the Near- and Middle East, Judaism, Christianity and Islam, have produced very clear statements on ethical issues, which have had an enormous effect upon the lives of people. If the diversification of religion continues, and the great religions of the world succumb to the pressures of social change, then one result may be a greater variation in moral principles. On the one hand, this could result in a more tolerant world, since there would be no definite, absolute yardsticks against which to measure behaviour and attitudes. On the other hand, it may lead to a world in which ethical values are diluted, and in which people have less and less recourse to ethical principles when deciding upon a course of action.

Griswold (1994, p. 110) describes the postmodern world as providing a 'sense that life is meaningless and culture only a play of images without reference to some underlying reality'. One of the features of the postmodern world is that the exponentially enhanced systems of mass communication have introduced great variety in terms of consumer goods, ideas, educational opportunities and information. Such a plethora of choice, wonderful at first, can perhaps be understood as having generated a sense of meaninglessness. In a world where everything is apparently available, what can be designated as special any more? What is more, this diversity is presented as a series of attractive images, of superficially exciting brands, products and artefacts, but which, as we scratch the surface, lack depth and substance. It is rather like gazing at a night-time scene in downtown New York or Shanghai. One's senses are assailed by the neon images, yet behind them all one suspects there is nothing of substance. In such a world which is apparently meaningless, it is understandable that people should search for a spirituality with which they can interpret the world. Yet there is the danger that this plethora of new religious movements should also lack substance, and equate to the neon advertising panels of a large metropolis. They seem attractive on the surface, but as one searches beneath, there is a lack of depth. This is the danger. It may not apply to all, but such an analysis provides a way of thinking about the kind of religious innovation which is being experienced in contemporary society.

Not only is it argued that postmodernism is typified by an absence of depth in terms of ideas and knowledge, but that it is also characterized by a merging on the surface of ideas from many different sources. These sources might be as varied as religious art from the medieval period, abstract sculptures on a religious theme, or hymns accompanied by the electric guitar in a contemporary church setting. The postmodern world, it is sometimes argued, no longer recognizes or respects distinctions between ideas or cultural traditions. In discussing postmodernism, Sarup (1993, p. 132) speaks of 'the deletion of the boundary between art and everyday life; the collapse of the hierarchical distinction between élite and popular culture; a stylistic eclecticism and the mixing of codes'.

DIVERSITY AND ECLECTICISM

Certainly many of the new religious movements which are focused on Eastern religious traditions are very eclectic in their approach, drawing upon Zen and other Buddhist schools, Hinduism and Taoism, not only for examples of formal scriptural teaching, but also for meditational and yogic techniques. In addition, the New Age movement is perhaps archetypally syncretistic in its approach, linking Wicca, Druidism, the use of crystal energy, yoga and Tantra, and many other approaches. The approach of postmodern religion is that there is no reason not to do this. One philosophical underpinning to this eclecticism is the notion that there are many different routes to religious experience, and many different ways to experience the Divine. One criticism sometimes voiced against the long-established religions is that either implicitly or explicitly, they can tend to imply that each is the best way to find God or to gain some spiritual realization. Even if this is not stated overtly, if members come to believe this, then it does tend to separate and divide people, rather than emphasizing their shared religious experience. There is a sense in which some people belong to a particular tradition, while others are excluded, and are therefore 'different'. Once extended into the wider society, such a religious philosophy can be divisive rather than encouraging of a shared community of human beings.

The philosophy of eclecticism, however, rests upon the assumption that it is in principle feasible to draw upon religious teachings from wherever desired, and to synthesize them into a coherent whole. There is no reason, according to this philosophy, for human beings to have to take a religion *in toto*; one can select those elements which one finds either useful or inspiring, and blend them into a personal faith. Taken to an extreme, however, it is difficult for such personalized religions to create religious communities, however small. At some stage, some people have to decide to be 'followers', in a tradition initiated by someone else.

Religious organizations have, with some exceptions, tended to be hierarchical and patriarchal in outlook. Those who are ordained have been the interpreters of the Divine for lay people. When the latter had a spiritual or other problem, lay people may consult the clergy. With a hierarchical system of clergy, it is as the clergy act as a conduit for both supplications, and for the word of God to be passed to religion members. Now the clergy within a religion have also traditionally acted as the guardians of the religious artefacts belonging to a tradition, of the rituals and ceremonies, and of the symbolism, whether real or implied, of a faith. Much of this material has often attained a high cultural status. Church choral music, Gregorian chant, religious poetry, the religiously inspired paintings of the Renaissance and religious sculpture have often been elevated in the public consciousness as having the status of 'high art' or 'high culture'. There has often been a distinction between the status of these cultural products and those of everyday culture. Yet the citizens of a postmodern world are less impressed by such distinctions, and are happy to draw upon any cultural product as long as it meets their needs, or they find within in, the requisite inspiration.

This is related to a very important philosophical and sociological question raised by Cowan and Bromley (2008, p. 231) who when discussing the question of how and by whom the status of a religion is determined, speak of 'the lived religious reality of practitioners who are not part of the power structure of the Church, but who derive significant spiritual benefits from their beliefs and practices'. The essential question concerns the mechanism by which a particular religion is validated by society, and agreed to be acceptable as a belief system. Traditionally such decisions have been taken by those in positions of power in society, whether holding political power or religious power. If a belief system was considered to be outside accepted norms of belief, then it was defined as a heresy, and the consequences for believers could be very severe indeed. However, the entire approach of this type of societal approval mechanism entailed people outside the religion which was being evaluated, passing judgement upon it. The evaluation was external.

As we enter the postmodern era, however, there is an increasing emphasis upon the social processes whereby individuals determine their own values, and indeed collaborate and interact, to make social life as they would wish it. People are generally no longer happy to permit the institutions of society to take decisions for them, but prefer to make their own decisions, particularly in relation to something as personal as religious faith. Hence, although it may be true that some new religious movements are in various ways, unusual and eccentric, on this perspective the members should be permitted to evaluate the religion themselves. The argument would be that it is the opinion of the members which matters, and not the value judgements of outsiders. Hence one criterion for evaluating new religious movements could be the degree of happiness and well-being generated by the organization. This would be a type of utilitarian moral judgement. If the majority of the members gain spiritual benefits, if they are happy being members and the organization generates feelings of well-being in members, then the movement would be judged to be acceptable. However, utilitarian arguments can be criticized on the grounds of an apparent pragmatism, which lacks absolute ethical criteria. Hence, it is possible that an organization may be acting unethically towards members, while the latter remain in general happy with the quality of their lives.

While individualism as a principle may at times seem attractive, linking as it appears to do with concepts such as personal autonomy and freedom, some writers have pointed out its logical limitations. Bruce (1995, p. 119) in discussing New Age religion, argues that '. . . New Age individualism inhibits the development of a body of shared values beyond those which allow individualism'. Now it could be argued that individualism is not in itself a value system of any kind; that it is merely a manner in which one may organize one's life. At the same time, even the most determined individualist would still need to take cognizance of at least some elements and limitations imposed by the general society. In terms of personal faith, any person may decide to be an absolute individualist and believe in any spiritual force, real or imaginary, that they wish. However, if the belief is so outlandish and unusual that no one else is prepared to give it any credibility at all, then it is ultimately likely to be a fairly limiting spiritual experience. It is only when we gather together, even in fairly small groups of like-minded people, that a spiritual belief system begins to take on some of the elements of a religion.

Certainly in a postmodern world, characterized by what one might term the fragmentation of existence, many would support in principle the notion of individual choice in questions of faith. However, when speaking of individual choice in terms of new religious movements, many would perhaps support the contention of Fisher (1999, p. 99) that '. . . the argument hinges on whether followers who exercise their choice can do so in an informed way and without undue coercion'. The question of access to information appears to be crucial here, and one can argue that this is one of the important elements of postmodernism.

Above all else, postmodernism has been, and is, the period of information dissemination, and the most significant change which has brought this about has been new technology. The computer and the internet have been probably the greatest influence, although satellite broadcasting and the mobile phone have played an enormous part. New religious movements have been able for the first time to reach an almost unlimited audience. They have been enabled to disseminate their religious viewpoints, to attract new members and subscriptions, and to bring their founders and teachers into direct contact with a large audience.

Crucially though, although the advent of the internet has enabled new religions to proselytize, it has also provided checks and balances upon their expansion. Those who are potentially interested in joining a new movement can use the internet to explore their ideas and philosophy, before they take the step of attending meetings and joining. They can reflect upon their religious ideas at leisure, and also compare their philosophy with those of other movements. They may thus be less likely to be swayed into a precipitate decision in terms of joining, than if they simply attended a meeting without prior information. The internet also enables potential members to email questions about the movement, and perhaps to challenge their ideas, before any commitment is made. In responding to such questions, the movement also has to commit itself in writing in an electronic communication of which there is a record. The result of this is that an openness of discourse is created, which is not only liberating for those involved, but it also tends to prevent undue influence being brought to bear upon people. Ideas can be challenged in an open way, and it is much harder for one person to overly dominate another, by virtue of their personality or charisma. What Featherstone (1995, p. 102) refers to as '. . . the universalizing

169

processes of the new communications technology' enables anyone to compare new religious movements, and encourages the free flow of information. Many religious organizations, and indeed many perfectly reputable ones, sometimes discourage participants in retreats and residential meditation seminars from bringing mobile phones with them. This is often justified by the argument that it is an intrusion upon the atmosphere of quiet contemplation and reflection which is necessary at such an event. On the other hand, one might argue that any limitation placed upon the free availability of information and communication is undesirable.

The ready availability of information technology, and the accompanying access to information in the postmodern age, encourages a consumer approach to religion. The person interested in religion potentially has all of the requisite information to select aspects which interest them from different religions. It is possible to create one's own religion, and then re-create it innumerable times, as one's interests change and evolve throughout life. This is in many ways an attractive proposition, but there is an inherent flaw in terms of the way in which religious ideas are communicated, particularly within the educational system. Hunt (2005, p. 41) argues that 'the difficulty is that without institutional expression and belief codes it is practically impossible to sustain doctrinal systems over the generations . . .'.

In a world in which there is a proliferation of individualistic or small group religions, it would become extremely difficult to teach these in a coherent manner in our educational system. At the moment normally only the major world faiths are discussed in schools, along with some variants. This becomes possible because each faith can be summarized relatively briefly in terms of its principal tenets and doctrines. It is, therefore, possible to present these religions to pupils in a coherent manner. This is an important task as it helps to inculcate or reinforce the idea that human beings are spiritual creatures. Arguably, we need to teach children about religious concepts if they are to retain a religious dimension to their lives in adulthood. This becomes even more important if this religious transmission is to continue from generation to generation.

In the case of new religious movements which are on a fairly small scale in terms of adherents, it is often the case that they do not develop extensive ceremony or ritual or other formal types of religious expression, nor do they necessarily develop scriptures or other written types of belief. The ideology or doctrine of the movement may not be fully developed, and certainly not committed to writing. Hence, it can be difficult in principle to determine exactly what the movement stands for, and also how one might go about teaching it in schools, colleges or universities. The leader of the movement may be the principal factor in determining the belief system, and as that leader changes, then the belief system may also be transformed. There are thus considerable difficulties in imagining how some new religious movements may progress to the next generation, or how the teachings may be transmitted into the future. If this dispersed, fragmented view of the way in which religion might develop is correct, then it is difficult to imagine where this might develop in the future. Previously, the major religions relied upon their key institutions, such as churches, to ensure the continuity of a social and religious structure, and also upon the teachings of the faith, usually enshrined in scripture, in order to enable the religion to be taught to future generations. With the advent of the internet, this mechanism may not prove to be so necessary, and electronic dissemination may be sufficient to ensure the continuity of faith.

The disaggregation of knowledge, and its rapid electronic dispersion, can generate a wonderful sense of freedom. People are no longer constrained by the doctrines and dogmas of traditional belief systems. However, within this new dawn of personal freedom, the storm clouds of uncertainty are gathering on the horizon. Aldridge (2000, p. 185) argues that 'radical doubt is always with us, insinuating itself into every corner of the life-world'. Perhaps the greatest uncertainty is that expressed in the nineteenth century by Nietzsche, the idea that we can no longer turn to God with our doubts and fears. One can argue that there has been a slow transition to a more secular society in the West, although this has been accompanied by the diversification of religious practice and belief. Overall though, it would appear that postmodernism is characterized by the ability and willingness of people to challenge the sacred truths of past years. The result is a tendency to lose the central values and certainties to which citizens have traditionally turned in times of crisis. It is difficult to predict the nature of the outcome of this, both for society in general, and for the future of religion.

Although many people in the postmodern world have opted to join new religious movements, others have taken a different, arguably more radical, stance. Although new religious movements may be unusual, unconventional, iconoclastic and subversive, in relation to traditional religious practice, they do in fact still share one element in common with older faiths. This is that they involve a community of people who by and large share a common belief system, whether that has slowly evolved, or has been created by the founder of the movement. There is at least a feeling of group identity.

However, some people within postmodernity have adopted a very different path. They have essentially committed themselves to an isolated, individualistic religious experience. There is a long-standing tradition of the religious seeker, living an individual life, usually in a remote area of desert, forest or mountains. The early Christian Desert Fathers, Sufi mystics, Hindu sadhus living in Himalayan caves and devotees of yoga have all practised this type of tradition. In some cases, they would belong to an established religious tradition, but have decided to live a life withdrawn from the world. The purpose of their withdrawal from the world would, in such a case, be to practise their devotions in a tranquil location where they could experience God or the Ultimate more intimately. In some cases, however, the person withdrawing from the world would be more interested in the perfection of the self, rather than devotion to God. There is evidence that the idea of individualistic religious experience, of not choosing to belong to a group or movement, is an attractive proposition for some people in contemporary society. Certain traditions, such as Paganism, Wicca, various mystical traditions, yoga and New Age, lend themselves to this type of religious experience. Such people are demonstrating the highly personal nature of some religious experience, in effect arguing that it is not necessary to share religious experience in a communal context. The individual religious person who combines elements of different faiths, or perhaps simply follows a single tradition, is arguably the ultimate example of the religious consumer in the spiritual market place. In such a case, the individual makes a selection of spiritual beliefs and practices, which are entirely devoted to self-realization, rather than to the good of the community.

CONCLUSION

Perhaps the ultimate question for new religious movements, and indeed for established religions, is whether the world in postmodernity is destined to become largely secular. If human beings are no longer prepared to accept the idea of 'meta-narratives', and want a world of individual choice, the logical development is towards an increased fragmentation or individualization of belief. To take the argument to its limits, this may mean more and more people developing their own, personal belief system, and the decline of religious organizations, whether traditional or in the form of new religious movements. Whether the ultimate extension of this is towards a secular state is a matter of debate. However, there is evidence that hints at a spirituality deep within the human condition; a spirituality which is inseparable from the very nature of what it means to be human. The cave paintings of the Stone Age suggest a representation of the spirit of the animals portrayed, and in ancient burial sites, the vestiges of ritual suggest a sense of the spiritual at the moment of leaving this earth. It may be over-emotive to suggest that spirituality and humanity are inexorably linked, but if so, then new religious movements are merely a manifestation of an eternal search for meaning in our transitory lives.

FURTHER READING

Ellwood, R. S. (1994) *The Sixties Spiritual Awakening: American Religion Moving from Modern to Postmodern*, New Brunswick: Rutgers University Press.

Heelas, P. (ed.) (1998) *Religion, Modernity and Postmodernity*, Oxford: Blackwell.

Lynch, G. (2007) *New Spirituality: An Introduction to Belief beyond Religion*, London: I.B. Tauris.

Lyon, D. (2000) *Jesus in Disneyland: Religion in Postmodern Times*, Cambridge: Polity.

Oliver, P. (2010) *Foucault: The Key Ideas*, London: Hodder Education.

GLOSSARY

Ahimsa: Hindu doctrine of non-violence

Apocalypse: a dramatic event in the future which will
                         lead to the end of the world

Autonomy: the capacity for independent, rational thought

Bhagavad Gita: widely read Hindu scripture; part of the
                         much longer Mahabharata

Bhakti movement: devotional School of Hinduism

Brainwashing: a psychological process whereby someone's
                         previously held beliefs are largely eradi-
                         cated and replaced by new beliefs

Charismatic leader: a person who by virtue of personality or
                         other qualities is capable of exerting great
                         influence over their followers

Cult: a completely new religious movement which
                         has only tenuous connections with previ-
                         ously existing faiths

Doctrine: a body of teaching

Enlightenment: the achievement of which can be said to
                         be the ultimate purpose of Buddhism; the
                         capacity to understand the true nature of
                         the world and of existence

Existentialism: school of philosophy often associated with
                         Jean-Paul Sartre and Simone de Beauvoir,
                         which asserted that the nature of human
                         existence was not preordained, but could
                         be determined by the individual

Heresy: opposition to an accepted belief system or
                         faith; the holding and articulation of such
                         opposing views

Ideology:	a world view to which its advocates are wholeheartedly committed
Indoctrination:	the process whereby people come to believe unshakably that something is true
Koan:	puzzling saying used as the basis of meditation in Rinzai Zen Buddhism
Millennialism:	the belief that the world will experience 1,000 years of peace and tranquility
Moksha:	Hindu term meaning release from the cycle of rebirth
Norms:	standards or values which may be used as the basis of judgements
Sadhu:	a wandering Hindu holy man
Sannyasin:	Hindu renunciant
Sect:	a religious movement which has broken away from a larger faith, but which retains fairly orthodox practices
Social construction:	the assertion that society and in particular knowledge is continually being created by the interaction of human beings.
Sufism:	the mystical element in Islam
Syncretism:	the blending together of ideas from different perspectives in order to construct a cohesive world view
Tao:	the Taoist 'Way' or spiritual force which pervades the universe
Theravada Buddhism:	the School of Buddhism found in South-east Asia, for example in Sri Lanka and Thailand, and whose scriptural language is Pali
UFO movement:	('unidentified flying object') the belief that advanced civilizations in other parts of the universe have made contact with the Earth, and that these contacts are generally benign
Vinaya:	Buddhist monastic code of conduct
Yule:	in Paganism, the festival of the Winter solstice

BIBLIOGRAPHY

Agne, R. R. (2007) 'Reframing practices in moral conflict: interaction problems in the negotiation standoff at Waco', *Discourse and Society*, 18:5, 549–78.

Agne, R. R. and Tracy, K. (2001) ' "Bible babble": naming the interactional trouble at Waco', *Discourse Studies*, 3:3, 269–94.

Aldridge, A. (2000) *Religion in the Contemporary World: A Sociological Introduction*, Cambridge: Polity.

Arlandson, J. (2007) 'Postmodernism and the Bible: introduction', *American Thinker*, 17 March, p. 3 [online] available at www.american-thinker.com

Avalos, H. (2001) 'Maria Atkinson and the rise of Pentecostalism in the U.S.-Mexico Borderlands', *Journal of Religion and Society*, 3, 1–20.

Bader, C. and Demaris, A. (1996) 'A test of the Stark-Bainbridge theory of affiliation with cults and sects', *Journal for the Scientific Study of Religion*, 35, 285–303.

Bainbridge, W. S. and Stark, R. (1979) 'Cult formation: three compatible models', *Sociological Analysis*, 40:4, 283–95.

Barker, E. (1984) *The Making of a Moonie: Choice or Brainwashing*, London: Blackwell.

Baumann, M. (1998) 'Working in the right spirit: the application of Buddhist right livelihood in the Friends of the Western Buddhist Order', *Journal of Buddhist Ethics*, 5, 120–43.

Beckford, J. A. (1981) 'Cults, controversy and control: a comparative analysis of the problems posed by new religious movements in the Federal Republic of Germany and France', *Sociological Analysis*, 42:3, 249–64.

Bendle, M. F. (2005) 'The apocalyptic imagination and popular culture', *Journal of Religion and Popular Culture*, 11, 1–14.

Berger, P. L. and Luckmann, T. (1967) *The Social Construction of Reality*, Anchor: New York.

Bird, F. (1979) 'The pursuit of innocence: new religious movements and moral accountability', *Sociological Analysis*, 40:4, 335–46.

Bird, F. B. and Westley, F. (1985) 'The economic strategies of new religious movements', *Sociological Analysis*, 46:2, 157–70.

Björkqvist, K. (1990) 'World-rejection, world-affirmation, and goal-displacement: some aspects of change in three new religious movements of Hindu origin', in N. Holm (ed.), *Encounter with India: Studies in Neohinduism*, Turku, Finland: Åbo Akademi University Press, 79–99.

Brear, A. D. (1996) 'The authority of Pramukh Swami within the Swaminarayan Hindu Mission', *DISKUS*, 4:1, 23–33.

Bruce, S. (1995) *Religion in Modern Britain*. Oxford: Oxford University Press.

Chin, S. S. (2006) 'I am a human being, and I belong to the world: narrating the intersection of spirituality and social identity', *Journal of Transformative Education*, 4:1, 27–42.

Chryssides, G. D. (1996) 'New religions and the internet', *DISKUS*, 4:2, 1–11.

—(2001) 'Unrecognized charisma? A study of four charismatic leaders', paper presented at the 2001 International Conference 'The Spiritual Supermarket: Religious Pluralism in the 21st Century', London, April, 2001

Collins, D. (2000) 'Virtuous individuals, organizations and political economy: a new age theological alternative to capitalism', *Journal of Business Ethics*, 26, 319–40.

Commission on New Religious Movements (1998) *In Good Faith: Society and the New Religious Movements,* Stockhom: Commission on New Religious Movements, the Government of Sweden.

Cosgel, M. M. (2001) 'The commitment process in a religious commune: the shakers', *Journal for the Scientific Study of Religion*, 40:1, 27–38.

Cowan, D. E. (2002) 'Exits and migrations: foregrounding the Christian counter-cult', *Journal of Contemporary Religion,* 17:3, 339–54.

Cowan, D. E. and Bromley, D. G. (2008) *Cults and New Religions: a Brief History*, Malden, MA: Blackwell.

D'Andrea, A. (2007) 'Osho International Meditation Resort (Pune, 2000s): an anthropological analysis of sannyasin therapies and the Rajneesh legacy', *Journal of Humanistic Psychology*, 47:1, 91–116.

Dawson, L. L. (1998) 'Anti-modernism, modernism, and postmodernism: struggling with the cultural significance of new religious movements', *Sociology of Religion,* 59:2, 131–56.

Dein, S. and Littlewood, R. (2005) 'Apocalyptic suicide: from a pathological to an eschatological interpretation', *International Journal of Social Psychiatry*, 51:3, 198–210.

Downing, M. (2001) *Shoes Outside the Door: Desire, Devotion, and Excess at San Francisco Zen Center*, Washington, D.C.: Counterpoint.

DuPertuis, L. (1986) 'How people recognize charisma: the case of darshan in Radhasoami and Divine Light Mission', *Sociological Analysis*, 47:2, 111–24.

Eisenhart, C. (2006) 'The humanist scholar as public expert', *Written Communication*, 23:2, 150–72.

Exon, B. (1995) 'Self-accounting for conversion by Western devotees of modern Hindu religious movements', *DISKUS*, 3:2, 74–82.

Featherstone, M. (1995) *Undoing Culture: Globalization, Postmodernism and Identity*, London: Sage.

Festinger, L., Riecken, H. and Schachter, S. (2008) *When Prophecy Fails*, London: Pinter and Martin.

Fisher, M. P. (1999) *Religion in the Twenty-first Century*, London: Routledge.

Geaves, R. A. (1996) 'Baba Balaknath: an exploration of religious identity', *DISKUS*, 4:2, 1–12.

—(2009) 'Forget transmitted memory: the de-traditionalised "religion" of Prem Rawat', *Journal of Contemporary Religion*, 24:1, 19–33.

Griswold, W. (1994) *Cultures and Societies in a Changing World*, Thousand Oaks, CA: Pine Forge Press.

Guest, T. (2005) *My Life in Orange*, London: Granta.

Hargrove, B.(1978) 'Integrative and Transformative Religions', in J. Needleman and G. Baker, *Understanding the New Religions*, New York: Seabury, 257–66.

Harrington, M. (2000) ' "Conversion" to Wicca', *DISKUS*, 6, 1–11.

Healy, J. P. (2010) 'Schisms of Swami Muktananda's Siddha Yoga', *Marburg Journal of Religion*, 15, 1–15.

Heelas, P. (1996) *The New Age Movement*, Oxford: Blackwell.

Holden, A. (2002) 'Returning to Eden: futuristic symbolism and its effects on Jehovah's Witnesses', available online at http://www.comp.lancs.ac.uk/sociology/papers/Holden-Returning-To-Eden.pdf (accessed 22 June 2010).

Hunt, S. (2005) *Religion and Everyday Life*, Abingdon, Oxon: Routledge.

Johnson, D. P. (1979) 'Dilemmas of charismatic leadership: the case of the People's Temple', *Sociological Analysis*, 40:4, 315–23.

Kent, S. A. (1999) 'The creation of "religious" scientology', *Religious Studies and Theology*, 18:2, 97–126.

Kent, S. A. and Hall, D. (2000) 'Brainwashing and re-indoctrination programs in the Children of God/The Family', *Cultic Studies Journal*, 17, 56–78.

Knott, K. (1993) 'Contemporary theological trends in the Hare Krishna Movement: a theology of religions', *DISKUS*, 1:1, 32–44.

Lewis, J. R. (2000) 'Sect-bashing in the guise of scholarship: a critical appraisal of select studies of Soka Gakkai', *Marburg Journal of Religion*, 5:1, 1–11.

—(2004) 'New religion adherents: an overview of Anglophone census and survey data', *Marburg Journal of Religion*, 9:1, 1–17.

—(2006) 'New data on who joins NRMs and why: a case study of the Order of Christ/Sophia', *Journal of Alternative Spiritualities and New Age Studies*, 2, 91–104.

Lyotard, J-F. (1986) *The Postmodern Condition: A Report on Knowledge*, trans. Bennington, G. and Massumi, B., Manchester: Manchester University Press.

Milne, H. (1987) *Bhagwan: The God that Failed*, New York: St Martins Press.

Nicolas, P. S. (2007) *A New Religious Movement in Singapore: Syncretism and Variation in the Sai Baba Movement*, Singapore: National University of Singapore.

Palmer, S. J. (1988) 'Charisma and abdication: a study of the leadership of Bhagwan Shree Rajneesh', *Sociological Analysis*, 49:2, 119–35.

Prather, C. H. (1999) 'God's Salvation Church: past, present and future', *Marburg Journal of Religion*, 4:1, 1–18.

Rambo, L. (1998) *The Psychology of Religious Conversion*, paper given at the International Coalition for Religious Freedom Conference, 'Religious Freedom and the Millenium', Berlin, 29–31 May, pp. 1–4.

Ren, P. (2007) 'Exploring a church of new Chinese immigrants in Southern California', *Marburg Journal of Religion*, 12:1, 1–25.

Richardson, J. T. and Introvigne, M. (2001) ' "Brainwashing" theories in European parliamentary and administrative reports on "cults" and "sects" ', *Journal for the Scientific Study of Religion*, 40:2, 143–68.

Saeed, A. (2007) 'Malcolm X and British Muslims: a personal reflection', *Journal of Religion and Popular Culture*, 16, 1–15.

Saliba, J. A. (1999) 'The earth is a dangerous place – the world view of the Aetherius Society', *Marburg Journal of Religion*, 4:2, 1–19.

Sarup, M. (1993) *An Introductory Guide to Post-Structuralism and Postmodernism*, Hemel Hempstead: Harvester Wheatsheaf, 2nd edn.

Shah, A. M. (2006) 'Sects and Hindu social structure', *Contributions to Indian Sociology*, 40:2, 209–48.

Shupe, A. D. and Bromley, D. G. (1979) 'The Moonies and the Anti-Cultists: movement and countermovement in conflict', *Sociological Analysis*, 40:4, 325–34.

Siegel, P. and de Barros, N.F. (2009) 'Yoga in Brazil and the National Health System', *Complementary Health Practice Review*, 14:2, 93–107.

Singer, M. T. and Lalich, J. (1995) *Cults in Our Midst: The Hidden Menace in Our Everyday Lives*, San Francisco: Jossey-Bass.

Srinivas, S. (1999) 'Sai Baba: the double utilization of written and oral traditions in a modern South Asian religious movement', *Diogenes*, 47:3, 88–99.

Stark, R. and Bainbridge, W. S. (1996) *A Theory of Religion*, New Brunswick, NJ: Rutgers University Press.

Sutcliffe, S. (1995) 'The authority of the self in New Age religiosity: the example of the Findhorn Community', *DISKUS*, 3:2, 23–42.

Swatos, W. H. and Christiano, K. J. (1999) 'Secularization theory: the course of a concept', *Sociology of Religion*, 60:3, 209–28.

Szerszynski, B. (1992) *Religious Movements and the New Age: Their Relevance to the Environmental Movement in the 1990s*, Lancaster: Centre for the Study of Environmental Change, Lancaster University.

Tidball, K. G. and Toumey, C. (2007) 'Serpents, sainthood, and celebrity: symbolic and ritual tension in Appalachian Pentecostal snake handling', *Journal of Religion and Popular Culture*, 17, 1–23.

Trevithick, A. (2008) 'The Theosophical Society and its subaltern acolytes (1880–1986)', *Marburg Journal of Religion*, 13:1, 1–32.

Upal, M. A. (2005a) 'Towards a cognitive science of new religious movements', *Journal of Cognition and Culture*, 5:1–2, 214–39.

—(2005b) 'Simulating the emergence of new religious movements', *Journal of Artificial Societies and Social Stimulation*, 8,1 [online] available at http://jasss.soc.surrey.ac.uk/8/d1/6.html (accessed 22 June 2010).

Wagar, S. (2009) 'The Wiccan "Great Rite" – *Hieros Gamos* in the Modern West', *Journal of Religion and Popular Culture*, 21:2, 1–38.

Wallis, R. (1984) *The Elementary Forms of New Religious Life,* London: Routledge and Kegan Paul.

Walsh, Y. and Bor, R. (1996) 'Psychological consequences of involvement in a new religious movement or cult', *Counselling Psychology Quarterly,* 9:1, 47–60.

Whitsett, D. and Kent, S. A. (2003) 'Cults and families', *Families in Society: The Journal of Contemporary Human Services,* 84:4, 491–502.

Wilson, B. R. (1993) 'The persistence of sects', *DISKUS,* 1:2, 1–12.

York, M. (1996) 'Defending the cult in the politics of representation', *DISKUS,* 4:2, 1–13.

—(2000) 'Nature religion as a contemporary sectarian development', *DISKUS,* 6, 1–10.

INDEX

Theravada Buddhism 79, 112
Thor 93
Tibetan Buddhism 85
Tolstoy, Leo 97
Triratna Buddhist Community
    77–80
typology 17

unidentified flying objects
    (UFOs) 21

vegetarianism 27
Venus, planet 22
Vinaya 79
Vorilhon, Claude 23

Waco siege 7, 59
Watts, Alan 100
Wicca 7, 18, 92

Zen 56, 134